ANGEL OF BATAAN

ANGEL OF BATAAN

The Life of a World War II Army Nurse in the War Zone and at Home

Walter M. Macdougall

Camden, Maine

Published by Down East Books
A wholly owned subsidiary of
The Rowman & Littlefield Publishing Group, Inc.
4501 Forbes Boulevard, Suite 200, Lanham, Maryland 20706
www.rowman.com

Unit A, Whitacre Mews, 26-34 Stannary Street, London SE11 4AB

Distributed by NATIONAL BOOK NETWORK

British Library Cataloguing in Publication Information Available

Library of Congress Cataloging-in-Publication Data

Macdougall, Walter Marshall.
  Angel of Bataan : the life of a World War II army nurse in the war zone and
at home / Walter Macdougall.
    pages cm
  Includes bibliographical references.
  ISBN 978-1-60893-374-7 (pbk. : alk. paper) — ISBN 978-1-60893-375-4
(electronic) 1. McAlevey, Alice Zwicker, 1917–1976. 2. United States. Army
Nurse Corps—Biography. 3. World War, 1939–1945—Medical care—United
States. 4. World War, 1939–1945—Prisoners and prisons, Japanese. 5. World
War, 1939–1945—Participation, Female. 6. Prisoners of war—Philippines—
Biography. 7. Nurses—United States—Biography. 8. Brownville (Me.)—
Biography. I. Title.
  D807.U6M217 2015
  940.54'7252092—dc23
  [B]
                                                              2015001653

Printed in the United States of America

CONTENTS

ACKNOWLEDGMENTS

This biography owes a great deal to Alice Zwicker's propensity for saving items and photographs. It was her nephew Rodney Tenney who saved Alice's collection and preserved it. However, Rod's role in creating this biography became far more than serving as conservator of the Zwicker Family Collection. He leant his extensive knowledge, judgment, ability as a researcher, and unfailing support to the writing of this book.

In addition to her insightful recollections of her Aunt Alice, Jayne Minchner Winters took on the proofreading of the text. For this arduous accomplishment, I am most grateful. Another of Alice's nieces, Lynn Zwicker Weston, took an active and helpful interest in this endeavor, as did her father, Eli Zwicker, who was Alice's younger brother. Eli had an exceptional memory and keen insights that he shared with me, along with his sense of humor.

Regrettably, Alice's brother Kenneth Zwicker died before I began researching this book. Nonetheless, I am deeply indebted to Ken, and I have often drawn from his delightful book, *Hard Times without Depression: Growing up in Maine 1920–1940*. Kenneth's wife, Marilyn Zwicker, has also been most supportive of this project.

Many of Alice's Brownville neighbors have contributed anecdotes, clippings, and photographs. When I was considering writing this biography, Carlson Williams, son of Alice's high school principal, and his wife, Carolyn, produced clippings and photos. Jane Macomber shared carefully saved letters from Alice about her operations. Ruth Barker described her training days at Eastern Maine General Hospital. Donald Stickney recalled Brownville in the time of Alice's youth, and local historian William Sawtell shared his long-standing interest in Alice's story. To all who helped, I offer my thanks. They have enriched my life as well as this book.

Help and encouragement came from far away as well as close at hand. I owe much to Mildred Dalton Manning, Alice's close friend, who was the last living member of the Angels of Bataan. Despite her physical condition, Mildred Manning sent me handwritten letters filled with recollections and invaluable information.

Deserving special thanks as well is Professor Elizabeth Norman, author of *We Band of Angels*, the definitive account of the nurses in the Philippines during World War II, who, despite her busy schedule, kindly gave advice.

Often people I met only by telephone went out of their way to track down information to answer my many questions. It is inspiring to know there are so many helpful and responsible people about.

The notes recognize the many sources and institutions that provided assistance. Among these are the Brownville Historical Society, the University of Maine's Special Collections, the MacArthur Institute, the American Defenders of Bataan and Corregidor, and the Center for Military History.

To all those mentioned above, to the many others who contributed and are not named, and to the entire Zwicker family, who permitted the writing of this account, I acknowledge my debt and express my thanks.

PROLOGUE

On February 5, 2013, the *Bangor Daily News* began its feature "Today in History" with the following item:

Today's Highlight in History:

On Feb. 5, 1945 . . . all Eastern Maine joined Mr. and Mrs. James Zwicker . . . in expressing pleasure and thanks that their daughter Lt. Alice Zwicker, Army Nurse Corps, had been freed from [an] internment camp at Santo Tomas in the Philippines.

This newspaper quote is overly conservative. In reality, *all* of Maine joined in welcoming Alice home. She was the only servicewoman in Maine who was a prisoner of the enemy in either of the two great world wars.

But there was more than that involved. Across the nation, whenever one of the seventy-seven Angels of Bataan returned home, there was a hero's welcome. Those army and navy nurses had shown what American women could do and be, even in times of defeat.

What follows is Alice's story—her childhood in a small Maine town, her commitment to the profession of nursing, and her immersion in World War II, including stints in Manila, Bataan, and Corregidor, followed by three long, hungry years when she was held prisoner by the Japanese.

For Alice, the terrible legacy of war did not end with her liberation from internment camp, or even with her homecoming. When Alice finally achieved victory, it was within her own soul. What is chronicled in the following pages is offered in honor of her compassion, her spirit, and her faith.

1

WHERE THE PLEASANT RIVER FLOWS

On one of the last, terrible days before Corregidor and those in Malinta Tunnel surrendered, Alice sat down to "breakfast" in the sifting concrete dust that fell with each pounding concussion from above. In her own words, there before her were "a tablespoon of cold corn beef hash on a dirty plate and half a glass of warm water in a dirty glass."[1]

In her mind she could visualize the wonderful spring near her home in Brownville, Maine. The fine sand at the bottom of that spring would move ever so slightly and continually as new, clean water from the earth bubbled upward, and the dipper that hung on a branch above the pool would be perfectly reflected upon the still surface.

It was the spring of home! Mixed with her hunger and exhaustion, thoughts of home came frequently. How gladly she would now contribute her alto voice to the church choir. What was that beautiful hymn with the Whittier words? "Within the Maddening Maze of Things," that was it:

> I know not where the islands
> Lift their fronded palms in air,
> I only know I cannot drift
> Beyond His love and care.

Alice had not given much thought to these words when she was a young choir member—probably few in Brownville did, young or old. However, on a December Sunday in 1941, all across America, the knowledge of geography suddenly expanded, and, in the days and months that were to follow, the faith of all would be challenged. The names and locations of many islands with fronded palms would become well known, and the losses in far-off places would anguish those at home. From the little village of Brownville and its surrounding country-side, 261 young people had gone off to war; thirteen would not return; and none would come home unchanged.

—◦✿◦—

For Alice, growing up in the 1920s and 1930s, the village of Brownville and its environs had existed largely as a world unto itself. One needs to visualize that place as it was to appreciate the magnitude of difference between it and the world into which Alice and many of Brownville's youth were to be hurled by World War II.

The village is divided by the Pleasant River, which flows down from what an early mapmaker called the Ebeemee Hills. More than hills, they are part of the Appalachian range, and from Brownville, their blue, rounded tops and long ridges command the northern horizon. From these mountains and their forests flows the river that gave the town its reason for being. Stand in Brownville Village, preferably on a quiet summer evening, and you will understand why people came to live in this place beside the river and between these flanking hills. What you will hear is the sound of waterpower. Up until recently, you heard the water racing down the sluiceways of a dam. Now the dam is gone, and you hear instead the river finding its way between and over the upturned ledges that rise like low, broken walls from the riverbed.

Not long before Alice was born, a person could be fined three dollars for not walking his or her horse through the covered bridge that connected the two parts of the village, one portion on the east bank of the river and the other on the west. The last of these barnlike structures spanning the Pleasant River at Brownville burned in 1915, the year before Alice came into the world. The replacement bridge was a structure of concrete arches, graceful and fireproof. On the west side of the river was the U.S. Peg and Shank Mill where, for many years, Alice's mother labored ten hours a day for ten cents an hour. Local people called it the Lewis Mill because it was owned by John Lewis, who had more money than most people could imagine.

When he was young, Eli Zwicker, Alice's brother, worked for John Lewis. One day Eli was smoking a cigarette while taking a break from bundling birch bars as they came from the saw. Mr. Lewis—people always referred to him this way—attired in his customary blue suit, came along and gave Eli a fatherly lecture on smoking.

"I know you come from a good family," Mr. Lewis said. "Those cigarettes aren't good for you, and besides, they waste a lot of time. Remember, a man should live to work and work to live." The latter was John Lewis's life view in one sentence.

The Lewis Mill had burned down in 1915, but it was rebuilt and added to until it stretched along the riverbank, both above and below the west entrance of the new bridge. South of the mill stood the Hotel Herrick, rising two stories above its surrounding porch; beyond the hotel you came to the Bangor and Aroostook Railroad station.

Having crossed the bridge to the east bank of the river, you entered the square, which was surrounded on the north and east sides with closely placed, two-story buildings and stores. On the south, the square was overshadowed by the Briggs Block. The first floor of this four-story building was occupied by shops that gave the square a progressive flourish when their window canopies were unfurled. The public library was located on the second floor of the Briggs Block, while the Freemasons and the Order of the Eastern Star had their hall on the third floor, with their kitchen and dining room on the fourth. Boys could earn five cents by carrying armloads of wood up four flights of stairs from the cellar and stacking it in the room next to the kitchen stove.

Alice and her sisters were asked to sing at special programs for the Eastern Star and for other village occasions, especially church functions.

The latter performances were obligatory. James (or "Jim," as he was known) and Mary Zwicker, Alice's parents, were too busy raising and supporting a family to belong to any of the town's many organizations, with one major exception: the Congregational Church, where James Zwicker was a deacon.

On the south side of the square, Pleasant Street entered close beside the Briggs Block. Tree-arched Pleasant Street kept company with the river. There were some larger houses along this dirt road, and it had a certain feeling of dignity, as befitted what had been the first road into the village. Throughout much of Alice's childhood, the Zwickers lived on Pleasant Street. Until Alice was in high school, the family lived in a house owned by Dr. Nathaniel Crosby, who was from a well-known medical family in the Brownville area. Dr. Crosby's father had been a Civil War surgeon. Crosby's practice was large; however, he charged two dollars for a house call, so the Zwickers did not often see him professionally.

When Alice was starting high school, Dr. Crosby decided to sell the house, and the Zwickers moved farther south on Pleasant Street, to a farmhouse that they rented for eight dollars a month. The square house was attached to a long ell and barn. Their only plumbing was a hand pump in the kitchen sink, but the house provided nine rooms and lots of space for a growing family. There was also room for a sizable garden between the house and the river, and that wonderful spring. This was the place that the Zwicker children remembered as home.

Running north from the square was Church Street, which climbed a long rise to reach the white Congregational Church at the top of the hill. From the church steps, the river valley is immediately to the right, or west. To the east is a large, bowl-like hollow. Eons ago, when the great ice sheet melted back to the Arctic, it left a wonderful place to play in Brownville—twisting eskers of gravel and sand, along with sizable depressions like the one to the east of the Congregational Church. Unromantically, and for reasons no one seems to remember, this depression was (and is) called Skunk Hollow. The hollow is a set-aside part of the village of Brownville. For a time, the Zwickers lived there before settling down on Pleasant Street. Alice's youngest brother, Eli, thought that his sister was born there.

Returning down Church Street, near the foot of the hill, there stood a large Grange Hall. Its auditorium seemed huge to Alice when she was a small girl. It was good-sized, able to accommodate the village's biggest social functions. When villagers reminisce about the hall, they remember sounds in particular: chairs scraping on the floor as a throng sat down to the church's "Old Home Day" suppers, raucous crowds at basketball games, and the contrasting solemn intonations of high school graduations.

Opposite this building, another road running east began its long climb up Stickney Ridge. On this road, a short distance from the corner with Church Street and at the top of the first steep rise, sat the school building that housed both the grammar and high schools. No one worried about physical education; the Zwicker children walked nearly a mile to school from their home on Pleasant Street.

A village is more than a place. Brownville was a tapestry of people, an interconnection of enterprises and relationships. Moreover, it was not as physically isolated as it might seem. The tracks of the Bangor and Aroostook Railroad, which followed the Pleasant River, carried daily passenger trains between Bangor and Aroostook County. Three and a half miles beyond the village of Brownville, at a place called Brownville Junction, the Bangor and Aroostook connected with the Canadian Pacific Railroad, whose rails, with a little help from the Maine Central Railroad, ran from the Atlantic to the Pacific coast.

Perhaps a thousand people lived in the township of Brownville. People knew their neighbors, even the more distant ones. Intercommunication thrived despite the scarcity of home telephones or cars. Like many families, the Zwickers did not have a car. There were so few automobiles that one of the boys in the Zwicker neighborhood memorized all the license plate numbers in town and could recite them upon request. People walked miles on errands, miles for pleasure, and miles to and from work. Walking meant meeting people or passing them as they sat on their front porches. Exchanging a few words was expected.

People went out of their way to get the local news and have a chance to talk. There was always a crowd that collected at the post office when it was time for the mail to be brought from the railroad station. Probably many present did not anticipate a letter. Daily routines and habitual practices, along with a goodly number of characters, were what Alice and her neighbors recognized as their hometown.

There was Steve Leach driving his meat wagon down Pleasant Street, or Jacob Larson delivering ice he had cut the winter before from the river above the dam. "I'll get you little 'swishers,'" he would say, pretending he was going to thrust long slivers of ice down Alice's brothers' shirtfronts. Then he would dole out ice for all the waiting children.

Earl Gerrish ran the general store located in the Briggs Block, a thriving business. Gerrish or one of his clerks went out and took grocery orders in the morning and delivered in the afternoon. One of his more distant customers once said he was sure that if he needed a yeast cake, Earl would bring it out. When asked, Earl's son said it was true; that particular customer had a big family that ate wagonloads of food over the course of a year.

Alice and her brother Kenneth were often sent to Gerrish's store with a grocery list, often written on the margin of a newspaper sheet.[2] In one of their mittens was the correct amount of change in pennies, nickels, dimes, and sometime quarters. Mr. Gerrish or his clerk, Thunder Melanson, would fill the order and wrap the items in brown paper ripped from the big, mounted roll on the counter. Ken and Alice used to watch Thunder when the item to be retrieved was a box on a top shelf. There was a special tool used in this operation—a pole with metal pincers on its top end that could be closed by a lever near the butt of the pole. Thunder would grasp the desired box with the pincers, turn around, release the box, and catch it behind him as it fell.

Now and then the mitten with the change would hold a surprise. Their mother would have put in an extra penny for candy, or sometimes Earl Gerrish simply decreed that there was a penny left over. Either way resulted in a hard decision. Should they buy two "Nut Twins" or three "Mary Janes" from the candy case?

When Kenneth Zwicker was in college and writing to Alice, it was their mutual experience of growing up in Brownville Village that provided a common text, a host of shared experiences that came alive with vivid references to childhood memories.

For instance, the place where Ken was boarding was like a certain Brownville neighbor's notorious, unkempt kitchen, or the living room of a well-known village bachelor, and it was noisy like the woman who could talk even loquacious Mrs. Carswell into the corner. Get two expatriated villagers together, and their conversation is colorfully full of real life, as only those with a similar upbringing can fully appreciate.

Quiet people with strong moral principles give a small town its solidity; characters who may have good values underneath, but are somewhat questionable on the surface, give a village its color.

John was an older man who boarded in the Elms House, situated on the east side of the square. John had taught his dog, Blitz, to hold a pipe in its mouth, and together they would sit on the boardinghouse porch and watch the doings in the square. When John spotted another dog, he'd say "Sic 'em" out of the side of his mouth. Blitz was a vicious fighter. Only one dog was his equal, a cocker spaniel that lived on Pleasant Street.

Unintentionally and innocently, it was the Zwicker kids who did away with Blitz's indomitable adversary. They had built a vehicle of sorts from a set of old wagon wheels. The ride down Pleasant Street, "hell-bent for election," as the saying goes, was exhilarating. There was no way to steer, which only added to the excitement. During one of the children's trips down the hill, the spaniel ran under a wheel and was fatally injured.

The Brownville reporter for the weekly *Observer* got paid by the inch, so it was fortunate for her that she routinely filled an entire column (and sometimes part of another) with local news. She included the names of anyone who participated in church programs or civil projects, attended birthday parties, or took part in school functions. It always pleased Mary Zwicker to see her name or the names of her children in the paper.

It is amazing how many families, including the Zwickers, had visitors from out of town, or went themselves to visit relatives. Travel accounts in the *Observer* diminished during the winter months, however, while news of the weather increased. The road up Stickney Hill was like a bottle with ice, while the growing thickness of the ice on the river meant ice jams and flooding in the spring. Cold weather and soot in the chimney also brought on the season of chimney fires. One early morning in February when it was fourteen degrees below zero, one of the Zwicker chimneys caught fire. Fortunately, the firemen had a chemical fire extinguisher, as water would have cracked the hot bricks.

Once in a while a reference in the local newspaper reminded the reader of Brownville's interesting ethnic mix.

The first settlers to the area were English stock from Massachusetts. They came seeking a chance to farm and to find prosperity in harvesting wood from the plentiful forests.

Then a dark band of high-quality slate that ran under the town was discovered. Welsh immigrants came and opened quarries that were situated on both sides of the river. There are slate gravestones engraved in Welsh in the Brownville cemetery. In 1930, when Alice was in high school, the Welsh still held a special church service during Brownville's Old Home Weekend. It was an occasion filled with music and the reading of Scriptures in their old language. Swedish men followed and found employment in the quarries, bringing their families. For a time, there were also black families whose menfolk worked in the quarries, but that was before the Zwickers' time.

—◦◦◦—

Alice was German on her father's side and Irish on her mother's. Like the town's entrepreneur, John Lewis, both of her parents came from Canada, her father from Nova Scotia and her mother from New Brunswick. However, unlike Mr. Lewis, both of her parents were poor when they arrived. According to family lore, James Zwicker trapped rabbits until he had enough money to come by rail from Nova Scotia to Maine. He never had enough money to go home, so the story goes.

It was in 1752 that the Zwickers came from Zeiskam, Germany, landing in the area of Lunenberg, Nova Scotia. Their passage was paid for, and their arrival part of a plan to balance the large French Catholic population with Protestants—in the Zwickers' case, Lutherans.

James Zwicker was born into a family of farmers in 1876. He had two brothers, one of whom became a successful farmer. The other showed the Zwicker grit and ingenuity; although he was blind, he was known for his ability to build perfectly square loads of straw despite its slippery nature.

James came to the Brownville area to work in the woods. His first job was as a sled tender. When empty log sleds returned to the logging operation to be loaded again, each set of sled runners had to be turned by sheer manpower. The sled tender lifted one end of the runners on his back and walked the runners around. It was tough work for any kind of money. James got eight dollars a month.

James revealed special skills when he got a chance to use them. He was a good carpenter and an expert saw sharpener, and he went to work for John Lewis using the latter ability. He worked at Lewis's sawmill, which had the unusual name of Kuroki and was located in the woods at an isolated spot on the Canadian Pacific Railroad, northeast of Brownville.

By this time James had met Mary, his future bride, and he was lonesome in Kuroki. As the days went on, he wished he had not left Brownville, where Mary was working. In one letter to her, James wrote that the woods were especially wet and that at the end of the day he "hardly had a dry stitch on." He was going to bed, wet clothes and all. He asked what sort of time she'd had in Milo on Friday night (evidently attending a dance or a social). He told her that he'd just read a story and fallen in love with the heroine, but the hero got there first. "That is like me," he wrote, "always behind." He signed his eight-page letter "Love from Jimmie."

Speaking with conviction, his son Eli said of James, "He was a good man." His son Kenneth wrote of him with affection, suggesting that his dad was possibly the "original God-fearing Christian."

Kenneth also recalls their father as a stoic man who kept his troubles to himself. Shortly after news broke of the Japanese attack on Pearl Harbor, Kenneth left for the Maine state capital and induction into the Marine Corps. His father, who was heading back to work as a carpenter at a Portland shipyard, rode with him as far as Augusta. Despite the fact that it was almost Christmas, it was a solemn trip. As the train passed through a drab winter landscape, inside, the two men faced the fear of the unknown. No one knew if Alice was alive or dead, and who knew what awaited Ken?

They fell silent. Ken's father looked steadily out the window. Finally he said, "We are almost in Augusta."

A young boy, peering at the two Zwickers over the back of his seat, turned to his mother and asked, "Why is that man crying?" Ken looked over at his dad and saw tears running down his face.

Alice's mother Mary Bartlett was born in 1884 in Chamcook, Charlotte County, New Brunswick. Her maternal grandfather was from Castledawson, Londonderry, Ireland, which partially explains why Mary was nicknamed "Irish." Mary had come to Brownville to work for Mr. Lewis. Her father had died, and she needed to support her mother. She and James Zwicker were married in May of 1912.

A neighbor recalled that Mary was "very lively, witty, and talkative." If her husband was quiet, Mary was spirited. She made it her practice to speak her mind. She may have had a touch of what the Gaelic people call "fey," for she could read tea leaves. There was always a teakettle and a teapot on the top of the big kitchen woodstove. When a neighbor stopped by, Mary would slide the teakettle onto the lid directly over the fire. After tea and talk, the guest's tea leaves would be read.

Alice's mother also had an uncommon number of sayings, such as, "If a broom falls across the door, then a visitor is on the way," or, "If your left hand itches, then you're going to come into money; if it's your right, then you're going to shake hands with a stranger." No one seems to have put much stock in these old sayings, but they were fun. One of her favorite expressions was, "Talk is cheap, but it takes money to buy the rum." Hearing her say this was surprising, because she was strictly against drinking spirits of any kind.

When Alice returned from the war, she said, "One thing I learned in the long years of waiting for release was what a mother truly means to one. . . . There is no one who can quite take the place of one's mother."

Mary's mother was a faithful Catholic, and seeing as there was no Catholic church in Brownville village, James Zwicker paid to have his mother-in-law driven to the one in Brownville Junction each Sunday. It cost him fifty cents a week, which was not small change when you were rearing a family on fifteen dollars a week or less. This reveals something about James Zwicker, as well as the bond he shared with his wife, Mary.

The Zwickers had to make their own way in Brownville. In all small towns, and perhaps especially in Maine, full "belonging" is often a matter of being born within the community. Unless you are born locally, one exists as both neighbor and "stranger," or perhaps as "neighbor on trial." This helps to explain why church participation meant so much to the Zwicker parents, and why the commendable performance of their children in church and school programs was so important to them.

All small villages have a certain air of openness—not necessarily of acceptance, but rather a quality that makes it difficult to hide your true nature. You do not grow up in such a village without discovering that human goodness often lives side by side with a small degree of human nastiness.

At the beginning of the war, James Zwicker was in the barbershop when something ugly was said to him about being a German. He never talked about this incident, but it hurt. Eli Zwicker remembers that in school he and his brother were called "Huns" and "Nazis" by some of their classmates. There is another fact about small villages that must be admitted: Inevitably there are some limitations when it comes to opportunities for realizing your potential.

But on balance, Brownville was a good place to grow up. In the midst of the Depression, being beside the Pleasant River, among neighbors, and exposed to an early demand for hard work and respon-

sibility provided essential nurturing for what lay ahead. Many of the
nurses who served with Alice on Bataan and Corregidor came from
similar rural environments. They testified that their early upbringing
and training had much to do with their survival and their performance
under terrible circumstances.

As a boy, Ken Zwicker used to wonder what brought so many people
back to Brownville for Old Home Sunday. He wrote: "Later, I understood why. There was no other place where they could visit with so
many old and dear friends; there was no other vacation place where no
one charged them higher prices in the summer. And there was no other
place where they knew such friendship and felt so welcome. There was
no other place where they were home."

2

GROWING UP IN BROWNVILLE

A lice Zwicker was born on August 6, 1916—a year when U.S. participation in World War I was darkly imminent, and, incidentally, the first year that Maine registered nurses. Alice was born at home, as were most babies of her generation. Although an attending physician signed her siblings' birth certificates, this was not the case for Alice. Times were hard for the Zwickers, and perhaps Grandmother Bartlett assisted in lieu of a doctor.

Alice was the third child, preceded by Catherine and James.[1] James died a year after Alice was born. In memory, he remained very much a part of the family. A little less than eleven months after Alice's birth, Gertrude Helena (by her own wish, the family called her Helena) was born. Three years later there was another boy, Kenneth Frasier, followed by Geraldine Louise; then, eight years after Alice's birth, came Eli Hibbert Zwicker.

There was a well-forged bond within the family. Scratch one, and you had all the others to deal with. Despite this "one for all and all for one" solidarity, there were contentions in the Zwicker household. Kenneth and Eli had a propensity for getting into scuffles with each other, especially after their mother had just gotten them presentable. For her part, Alice resented wearing Catherine's hand-me-downs.

Most important was the fact that their parents, although strict, loved their children. Years later, and shortly after Mary Zwicker had passed away, Alice wrote:

> Too many parents of our generation have determined that "My kids are going to have what I didn't have." . . . But they have missed one very important factor, and that is love in the home—even without money. . . . There was never a time when we didn't have plenty to eat and a clean bed to sleep in and clean clothes to wear—even if they had belonged to somebody else first! . . . I have dreamed of Ma nearly every night. . . . We didn't realize how hard it would hit us when she finally did die.[2]

Ken Zwicker described the years of his youth as "hard times without depression." Times were indeed hard, and became harder. Even the Brownville church had to privately borrow money to pay its minister. Through it all, Mary Zwicker kept her head held high, as the Rodgers and Hammerstein show tune admonishes us to do when times are dark.

In his writings, Ken calls his mother by her nickname, "Irish," as nearly everyone did, and he does so with admiration rather than with any disrespect. He remembers how, hours before morning light and before the rest of the family was up, Irish would be at work in the kitchen. Alice's father would laughingly complain that his wife banged pans just to keep him awake. But he was aware of what his wife did to keep the family going: cooking, washing, cleaning, and making clothes—all on top of working in the peg mill.

Her youngest daughter wrote these lines about their mother:

> Who is the finest one I know,
> Who never cared for pomp or show,
> But always hoed a hard old row?
> Who always cooked and sewed all day,
> Who stood all day over in the mill,
> With thoughts of many mouths to fill?
> Who has our love and always will?
> *My Mother*

Their mother was a no-nonsense, tell-it-as-she-saw-it person. According to family lore, when a teacher shook one of the Zwicker boys and tore his newly made shirt in the process, Irish arrived at school with a message: "I know you have to discipline my boys," she announced, "but from now on you are to take his shirt off before proceeding."

James Zwicker was used to "bone-weary work," to use an expressive old phrase. A year after Alice was born, he was walking or riding a bicycle three and a quarter miles to a job as a carpenter on a new YMCA building located in Brownville Junction. He was often away from home, working in the woods, and later on, he would be gone for considerable periods of time, laboring in a shipyard in South Portland, Maine.

James always seemed to work in an environment of risk. While working at Brawn's Sawmill south of the Brownville Depot, he lost two fingers and part of a third while running a notoriously dangerous snap-dragon saw. When the saw jammed, James tried to clear the blade, and his mitten got caught.

James was solidly against going into debt or even charging a few groceries to the store tab. He had a hole in his pocket one day and lost his change on the way to the store. He refused to take the groceries he had ordered. He returned down the road, found every cent in the dust, went back, and reordered. Alice was always taught to "pay as you go," and her father's resolve and endurance figured in her character.

Two years before Alice graduated from high school, her father had surgery in Bangor, Maine. The cost of the operation took all the money he had laid aside, and there was nothing left to pay for the required hospital stay. James refused to go into debt. He got dressed, somehow got to the railroad station, and took the 4:40 to Brownville. A neighbor saw him staggering up the station platform and, knowing that James Zwicker was not a drinker, realized that something was very wrong. He gave James a ride home. But the travail was not yet over, for when they arrived, they found that the Zwicker home had just been quarantined for scarlet fever. The Ladds, who lived nearby, took James in until the quarantine was lifted.

By necessity the Zwicker children grew up as hardworking members of the family. As they grew, each assumed part of the labor. Beyond working diligently to meet the needs of the family, however, there were other factors that knit this family together, and one of them was the sharing of music.

Their mother could play piano, but it was Catherine, Alice's older sister, who was the true pianist. A classmate wrote in their high school yearbook: "You should hear her tickle the ivories!" It was Catherine who usually played the old pump organ for the family sing-alongs. Alice also played piano impressively, but by ear. All you needed to do was hum a piece, and she could play it. Both she and Catherine received lessons for which their mother had somehow saved the money.

But Alice's training at the keyboard ended when her teacher left her to practice and came back to find Alice hammering out a jazzy version of "Barney Google (with the Goo-Goo-Googly Eyes)." The music teacher advised Mrs. Zwicker that she didn't think Alice was serious enough to continue.

Kenneth Zwicker recalled those evening sings with delight. Their parents would be sitting on the couch or in rocking chairs, making requests now and then. Years later he remembered all the words to the old songs they sang. There were old, sad songs: "The Dying Nun" and "Just Break the News to Mother"; he also remembered sheet music with romantic, dreamy pictures on their covers, like "Beautiful Ohio" and "Give My Regards to Broadway."

On Sunday evenings, only hymns were allowed. Eli Zwicker remembered "Whispering Hope": *Wait till the darkness is over, wait till the tempest is past*. That hymn offered wonderful opportunities for harmonizing, as did "Under His Wing." So many of the old hymns were fun to sing. One could set a rocking chair in motion to one of those gospel tunes. An in-law humorously remembers family members returning their traveling rocking chairs to their original positions on the linoleum floor after a stirring rendition.

The old Edison Fireside Cylinder Player was already an antique, but it gave the family countless hours of enjoyment. On the side of the machine was a picture of a dog listening intently to a large horn, just as the Zwicker children did. That horn fascinated Eli when he was small; it was attached to the needle and followed the grooves across the length of the cylinder. Besides musical numbers—"Teasing Moon," "The Bridal Chorus," and "Trail of the Lonesome Pine"—there were comedy sketches, such as "The Talk on Married Life" and a humorous account of a fellow who went down to New York ("Yack") City and didn't get to bed till 7:30 in the evening.

Children's programs at the church featured a great deal of music. They were serious events, especially for the Zwicker parents. As the children became older, they were given prominent parts. When they appeared on the church rostrum, it was family-on-review time. There was Children's Day itself, which came in June, when the children had plenty of time to practice and learn parts, and then there were "children's programs" at Christmas and Easter. When these programs went well, the world was good, and when things went wrong, it was shame on the family name.

When Alice, all dolled up in a costume, caught her heel on the edge of the rostrum carpet and tumbled down several stairs to the church floor, their father was mortified, while their mother prayed that a hole might open before her into which she, herself, could disappear.

Despite this event, the young Zwickers always answered the call of the theater. When she was in nurses' training in the 1930s and came back for Old Home Weekend, Alice was drafted to play the maid in *The Chintz Cottage*, a production that the *Piscataquis Observer* reported was "all that could be desired."

The family was literally on parade as they marched to and from church, walking two by two with their parents in the rear, to ensure there was no straggling. The girls were particularly conscious of their dress on these occasions. Standing on her front lawn, "Aunt Jean" Gerrish (like many families without relatives in the village, the Zwickers adopted aunts and uncles) would look them over as they trooped by. When she told Eli that he looked like a new dollar bill, Kenneth commented to Eli that he would never again be so highly complimented. (Aunt Jean was exceedingly careful with money. She once paid Eli $1.54 for sawing and piling seven cords of wood; the four cents, she said, was a tip for doing such a good job.)

At church, the family filled an entire pew. It could be an uncomfortable experience for someone new to the congregation should he or she decide to sit in what Irish considered the Zwicker family pew.

On the way back from church, they would usually go by way of the cemetery, where they would stop and visit the grave of little James. His grave was also a frequent stop on the family's less formal walks. Sometimes they deposited flowers they had made from papier-mâché and dipped in wax.

Mrs. Zwicker's excuse for taking family walks was that she liked to look at the houses and see what the neighbors were doing, but for a family with limited means of entertainment, those walks accomplished much more. One favorite route crossed the Pleasant River Bridge and continued west to the top of the hill and the white colonial house built by the original Brown of Brownville. The route then turned south and followed the road past the impressive Ryder place and the farm of the Bergman Brothers, who had more money than anyone guessed. There were stories to be told all along the way, and then there was a trail through the woods that ran diagonally down the ridge and back to the village. On this trail, they went single file, "like Indians."

Years later, memories of those summers came back to Alice like the happy aroma of raspberries in the warmth of sun. She remembered the coolness of Pleasant River when you waded and swam at the ledges and the excitement of furnishing a new tree house with comfortable cast-offs. On a Saturday trip to the tree house, you might bring thick slices of bread fresh from the oven and, as a special treat, share a quart jar of homemade root beer.

There was, of course, the garden with its seemingly interminable rows to be weeded on your hands and knees, but there were also expeditions where purposeful work merged with the better part of fun. Berry picking was one of these. When you heard Mother rattling pails in the pantry, you knew that such an adventure was in the offing. Mary Zwicker gave each of her berry pickers a pint dipper, which was less discouraging to fill. Dipper after dipper when full was dumped into a two-quart lard pail. When their mother was working at the mill, Catherine, as the oldest, was in charge of the expedition.

It was most fun when the whole family went berrying together. Expectations of pies and jars of jam on the shelf were enough to overcome their fear of bears, which everyone knew must be lurking somewhere in the blueberry patches. Though no one ever saw one, the possibility kept the children in a group. Sometimes James Zwicker walked his troop of berry pickers to an opening left by woodcutters. It was hard climbing over the crisscross of branches and limbs left behind, but they found abundant red raspberries there, enough for the family's "raspberry orgies."

Summer was also the season of thunderstorms. Grandmother Bartlett, a short, stout, Irish lady who lived with the family for a number of years, was in charge of what Ken Zwicker later described as "Operation Thunderstorm." The whole household (with the exception of their father, who refused to be bothered) would be rushed into the parlor and seated in a circle with whatever clothes they had not been able to get on piled in their laps. The sudden bursts of brilliant light momentarily illuminated the circle of faces while Grandmother, in a last precaution, sprinkled holy water on her grandchildren.

When the Zwickers were living in the Crosby house, each member of the family made his or her solo trip on the family bicycle perilously down the steep drive and straight into Pleasant Street. The older girls would hold the bike while a younger sibling climbed aboard, which wasn't all that difficult, as it was a girl's model—a fact that had not deterred their father from riding it to and from work in his earlier Brownville years.

The Columbia bicycle—already a rare antique when James Zwicker rode it to work—may have belonged to their mother when she was younger. It had wooden fenders and an unusual gear drive. Later, Kenneth and Alice used it to deliver papers in the snowless seasons. People would stop them to look at the bike more closely. Kenneth Zwicker wrote a rollicking account of his first descent on the bicycle, in which a neighbor's hen was nearly sacrificed and another neighbor almost drove his touring car into the ditch as he evaded the missile that shot from the Zwickers' drive.

Mary Zwicker came from a large family, including a sister who lived in southern Maine and whose children were older than Alice and her siblings. The house on Pleasant Street was a favorite place for the cousins to visit. Mary Zwicker always made them feel welcome, and she was, as everyone knew, an exceptional cook. The cousins contributed to the good family times. Artie, for instance, played the piano and brought with him new and sometimes questionable songs.

Thanksgiving was a special time, filled with good smells from the kitchen. Preparations began several days before the event, during which the girls were busy helping their mother. But there was always time for skating on the frog pond in Skunk Hollow. There, between sorties out on the ice, groups of young folk sat on logs around the fire. The older youths would try a kiss or two, while the younger ones took note.

The Zwicker brothers appreciated Thanksgiving—the food; the skating on the frog pond; and the end of the wood-sawing, -splitting, and -piling season. Their father believed that preparing the winter's firewood built character. There was plenty of opportunity, as the Pleasant Street house had five stoves, which turned sixteen cords of wood into ash each winter season.

Whether character was built or not, there were personal benefits from hot stoves in winter. Chief among these was getting your chance to dress by the one in the living room when the frost was thick on the windowpanes and winter held the world in its grip. Wood also fed the home's central feature, the kitchen stove. There was a large tank on the end of this stove where water was perpetually heating. On Saturday night, hot water would be ladled out of the stove's tank and poured into round, metal tubs for baths in two shifts—one for the girls and the other for the boys.

Only the worst winter weather kept the Zwicker children from going outside. Their father had built them two long sleds, which Geraldine remembered in a poem:[3]

> . . . a sight to behold,
> both beautifully carved with initials and moons,
> and we never minded the cold.

When the weather was too ferocious to go outside, there was always reading, and playing games; for a real treat, their mother would organize a taffy pull.

They all found ways to earn money, though it was harder for the girls, as babysitting was one of the few paying jobs for girls. Both sisters and brothers delivered movie theater flyers and sold items door to door. As salespeople, they earned prizes that were used as Christmas presents for their parents, and sometimes for themselves. They had to sell a prodigious quantity of Larkin Soap to earn a Morris chair as a prize, and a great many cans of Cloverine Salve to earn a banjo ukulele.

The biggest and most courageous of their childhood enterprises was Ken Zwicker's four-mile paper route. Alice was a participant in this venture, delivering to customers on one side of the river while her brother took those on the other side.

The paper route operation began at 3:30 a.m., when Train #1 dropped off a bundle of the *Bangor Daily News* at the Brownville Depot. In summer, it would be getting light, but during the winter, in the middle of a two-day blizzard, the situation was far different. Years later, Alice and Kenneth talked about that morning when the drifts were building in a world of cold and sweeping snow. They wondered just what difference it would have made if the papers had not been delivered that day. The railroad yard, which was close by the river and open to the wind, was a very cold place. (The record cold for Brownville was registered on the station thermometer at fifty-two below zero, Fahrenheit.) The section foreman had given them a chance to warm up by the stove in the base of the water tower before they started out with the papers. "You're grittier than hen manure, but not so strong," he told them as they ventured out into the frozen, dark morning.

Alice completed her half of the route, but Ken ran into real trouble when, mitten over his face as a shield, he tried a shortcut through an exposed and windswept area of Skunk Hollow. He reached a point in the drifts where he could not move; he was literally being buried. Mrs. Gould had been watching him through a window above her kitchen sink and came to his rescue with a teenage daughter and a shovel. When Mary Zwicker heard the story, her comment was, "The Good Man [God] just wasn't ready for you."

And then there was Christmas.

On returning from the Philippines, Alice remarked that she would like to live in the tropics, except for Christmastime. "Christmas without snow just isn't Christmas," she said. Fifty years later, Alice would write to her niece about the fleeting dreams she had of Christmas: "Carefree happy times going after the tree—little money, lots of love—fun before we grew up. I feel lonely for a few brief minutes," Alice admitted, reflecting on this bygone era.[4]

James Zwicker would announce that it was time to cut the Christmas tree, and the children would go out with him into a world of freshly fallen, crystalline snow. It was not a hurried adventure. They waited for the younger ones to catch up and shouted to each other when they thought they had found the perfect tree. But perfect trees, full and symmetrical and just the right size to almost reach the parlor ceiling, were not easy to find. One had to walk all the way around a tree and view it from all directions. In the end, it was their father and the elder sisters who made the final decision.

Back home, the evening would be occupied with decorating the tree. Red and green paper was cut into strips. Then their mother made wallpaper paste, and the strips were pasted together to form links. Link by link, the decorative chains were manufactured by the yard. And while that was being done, the wire basket corn popper was being shaken on the kitchen stove until, with a rattle of exploding kernels, white popcorn filled the popper. The popcorn provided material for more tree chains and for molasses popcorn balls. When these balls had been made, Catherine would sit down at the pump organ and they would sing carols, surrounded by the aromas of Christmas—the sprucey smell of the tree and the wafting spicy scent of pies baking in the oven.

There were no strings of lights upon the tree, but there was tinsel. Even on Christmas Eve, there were no presents under the tree. Gifts were hidden away to appear very early on Christmas morning, perhaps around 4:00 a.m., when Irish would start yelling "Merry Christmas!" from the foot of the stairs. There would be cocoa ready, their father would get the fire in the stove crackling, and it would be time to open presents.

When the children were young, their father made wooden toys for them. Irish was always knitting socks and mittens and secreting them away. There might be a glorious surprise: a big box weighted with a brick, just to fool the opener, and a small box inside with the item you had seen in the catalog and wanted so much—something their mom had saved pennies all year to buy.[5] Then Christmas was over, and school would begin again.

Like Christmas, schooling was important to Mary Zwicker and her husband.

When Alice's sister Helena graduated from high school and was not yet old enough to start nurses' training, she wanted to go into the mill to work. Irish said "no" as solidly as only she could. "You go into the mill and earn some money and get used to spending it, and you will never go on to school. You'll never get anywhere but married."

Mary may have had another reason for not wanting her daughters to work there. The mill was a firetrap, its wooden buildings filled with fine sawdust, its manufactured items polished with paraffin. Several years after Alice graduated from high school, there was a raging fire at the mill. No one was killed, but it was close. One girl had taken off her boots and had them under her workbench. By the time she found them after the call of "Fire!" rang out, there were sparks falling from the ceiling. There were all sorts of dangers in those Depression years, and education was the best insurance against them.

For Alice, school was more than just preparation for the future; it was also a social opportunity. Perhaps she was a bit too social at times, receiving a C in deportment as a first grader. There was a one-sided discussion at home, and that grade went to a B the next month, and then

A's for the rest of the year. Arithmetic was her weakness; she got two D's in that subject during third grade. Another talk must have occurred in the kitchen on Pleasant Street, for there followed five B's in arithmetic. Music and spelling brought straight A's.

The teacher's ranking on the attitudinal side of the report card is most interesting. Alice's teacher thought she was capable of doing much better; according to the check marks, Alice also was inclined to mischief and whispered too much.

A poem in the Brownville High School newsletter, *The Reflector*, written by Alice's sister Helena, conveys the same, if lighter-hearted, impression of Alice:

> Zwicker the dog and Stone the cat
> Side by side in High School sat,
> One nor the other had studied a wink.

"Zwicker" would be Alice, and "Stone" is doubtless her close friend and conspirator, David Stone. Despite this jibe, Alice was a solid B student in the college preparatory course, which included Latin and algebra. It should be added that she had plenty of competition. There was a group of bright young people in Brownville during Alice's high school years, including her older sister, Catherine, "who studied hard with lots of vim," as Catherine's yearbook reported. It was not easy to follow Catherine, who was editor of the yearbook, was voted class actress and artist, and then won the honor of being valedictorian of her class.

Those in Alice's class who were vying for top honor positions (valedictorian, salutatorian, first honor essay, and so on) were to be disappointed. On a brilliant moonlit night in March 1932, the Brownville School burned to the cellar hole, along with all the academic records, making the figuring of these top spots, which often involved tenths of a grade point, impossible. Incidentally, but adding irony, the firemen that night arrived at the fire barn to find that the town's Model T fire truck had four flat tires. Such things happen in a volunteer society. School was finished that year in the lobby of the Hotel Herrick.

During Alice's high school years, Mathew Williams, a gifted graduate of the University of Maine, became the principal of Brownville High School. He was still in his twenties and just married. His wife, Ruby, had been a teacher in the school where Mathew had taken his first job. The students in that school had referred to the couple as "principal and interest." In fact, Mathew and Ruby generated a great deal of interest in Brownville, daring to go on adventures like driving in a coupe car from Maine to the World's Fair in Chicago (the total gas bill for the trip was ten dollars, a hefty amount in those days). They had high aspirations for themselves and the village's young people.[6]

For Alice, the Williamses were part of a new excitement, an awareness of expanding possibilities and serious responsibilities to come. Before Alice graduated, a real friendship had evolved. After Alice returned from the war in the Pacific, she gave the Williamses an enlarged copy of her portrait as a newly commissioned captain, on which she wrote: "To the Williamses, whom I have known so long and liked so much. Much love, Alice."

Living in a rural area does not mean a poverty of experience or enforced isolation. Many cultural programs came to the village, including Whitefield Laile, a Bangor baritone who sang at the Grange Hall. On the program, there were selections from Handel and old favorites like "Londonderry Air." Perhaps of more importance than the programs performed for the villagers was the opportunity for participation. When Alice was in high school, students got to take part in formal debates, including one that asked debaters to "resolve that chain stores are detrimental to the interests of the public." Local disputes and interests may have been behind that topic of debate, but there are some larger social questions embedded in this issue that still have our attention today.

Nothing, not even salvation or dances, was more important in small towns like Brownville than sports. Most local towns had baseball teams; high schools in larger towns like Milo fielded football teams as well. The Swedes brought skiing to the area, and cross-country running had its following, but basketball was king of the heap. While athletic options for the girls were limited, Brownville High did have a girls' basketball team.

Judging from a photo, most of the high school girls were involved. No one wears a uniform in the photo, and there is no coach evident. Alice kneels in the front row with a basketball in her hands.

Alice was becoming aware of another world "out there." If local birthday parties, scavenger hunts, sledding outings, and trips to Milo when the carnival came to town were exhilarating, what must this bigger world offer? In the process of discovery, reading became important to Alice. It was a means of self-fulfillment, and it would be a way of survival in the tough times that lay ahead. Most important, Alice also discovered that she enjoyed doing things for others; she had always been helpful, just as she had always wanted to be a nurse.

Cousins weren't the only influence from the outside world. Alice's parents subscribed to the Bangor and county papers, along with the *Grit*, a national weekly aimed at the rural population.

Then there were the movies. Alice's first exposure to the drama and glamour portrayed on the silver screen was at the Brownville Grange Hall. A lot of people liked cowboy movies, including Alice's father. Older people in Brownville still remember cowboy actor Hoot Gibson. The films were silent, but Avis Price, a local high school girl, supplied lots of emotion at the piano. In the neighboring town of Milo, the Chic Theater featured "talking pictures" in the 1930s. Occasionally the Zwicker young people got to Milo, where they were introduced to the Hollywood world of furs, glitter, music, and dance. Barbara Stanwyck starred in *Night Nurse*, which played at the Chic in 1931. Whether Alice saw that film depends on whether her mother knew that it was considered risqué.

Not much escaped Alice's notice. There was so much that was interesting and fun—so much that was bubbling up around her, despite the economic Depression: swing music, the Lindy Hop, and an increasing availability and range of beauty aids, such as lipstick and nail polish in matching shades.

When the Zwicker children entered adolescence, it necessitated new family rules. There was more to the parents' concern than the threat of public humiliation, but all the same, it would have meant ruinous disgrace for the family if a daughter got in the "family way" before graduation. Irish repeatedly reminded her girls that "there was no trusting boys," and their father explained to every expectant boy who came calling that the Zwicker girls didn't date until they were eighteen (this supposedly got the girls safely through high school).

However, boys who passed scrutiny were allowed to call. On such occasions, at ten o'clock in the evening, Irish would come through the living room, go into the kitchen, and, while loudly winding the clock, announce, "Well, it's time for all decent people to be a-bed and rogues a-running." Boys got the message.

Despite the rules, Alice and her sisters found ways to "date." They would go to choir practice, get the numbers of the hymns for Sunday, and then take off with boyfriends for a walk. In a small town where gossip had wings, that sort of thing could not have happened on a regular basis.

By the time Alice graduated from high school on June 15, 1933, a new school building had been built; nonetheless, the ceremony was held at the Grange Hall to accommodate the large crowd of family and neighbors. High school graduations were big events in Brownville. The hall was decorated in the class colors of blue and silver. The class motto was displayed, backed with greenery: "We build the ladder by which we climb." When the curtain rose, the seniors were revealed, seated on the stage. Then the underclassmen entered the hall, singing a "song of presentation" and throwing flowers on the stage as they marched past. The seniors stood in the hush that followed and sang their "song of acceptance."

During the program that followed, Alice presented the class gifts. A week later the seniors went on their class trip: a long day's tour of central Maine, including the state capital and the University of Maine.

It was now the summer of 1933, and Alice would have to wait a year to enter the nursing program at Bangor's Eastern Maine General Hospital. She had outgrown the dark-rimmed glasses that had been one of those things to be endured during junior and senior high. She was now a striking young woman with brown hair, gray eyes, and a lovely, contagious smile. She was never a large person physically. Her uniform size was fourteen, and her shoe size, six. She was, however, big in spirit and vivacious on her feet. She did wish she was taller. She gave her full-grown height as "five feet, four and a quarter inches."

Alice, like most young people her age, left her home feeling a need for freedom. In simplest terms, she was fed up with dances at the Grange Hall encircled by watchful old people who shared her parents' anxieties.

Alice might not have realized it at the time, but she left the village of Brownville with a solid heritage. Her brother Ken spoke about that legacy when he wrote about kitchens, such as the one he and Alice had known on Pleasant Street:

> Those kitchens always smelled good. In the morning there was the pleasant aroma of bacon frying and coffee coming to a boil in the gray agate pot. . . . I realize it's just dreaming, but I've often thought that it might be a good thing if some of the world leaders whose countries can't seem to understand each other could sit down and talk things over some Sunday afternoon in a big, farm kitchen in New England. It's hard to believe that anyone in an environment like that could talk or think about anything except peace and friendship.[7]

3

THE FAR-OFF MAKING
OF A WORLD WAR

It's easy to imagine meeting Alice, her sisters, and their chums as they laughed and shared youthful gossip on their way to choir practice. As their laughter mixed happily with the warm air of a Brownville evening and the sounds of the Pleasant River, catastrophe was brewing on the international scene of political machinations and nationalistic ambitions. As yet, like a storm still far out to sea, the influence of this new human disaster had not greatly troubled much of America, but the storm was building—inevitably, it seems—and, when it finally came ashore, a generation of young men and women would be torn apart.

In the first quarter of the twentieth century, that storm was materializing across an ocean so vast that it covers over one-third of the planet. The very vastness of the Pacific created a false sense of security for those who wanted isolation. What was going on both ideologically and in reality seemed to most Americans the business of another world. Of course, there were those who sensed the consequences, who judged what was happening with moral compunction or with military alertness. They would try to avert war, or at least properly prepare for it, but their efforts seemed inextricably absorbed into a growing tragedy.

Looking back while writing his history of the war in the Pacific, Samuel Eliot Morison observed that peace in the Pacific might have been preserved if a way had been found to support the liberals in Japan. Morison realized that this was a huge "if." The roots of impending conflict ran long and deep into a "heart of darkness," to borrow Joseph Conrad's phrase.[1]

Alice's adult life was shaped by being plunged into a conflict not of her own making. This chapter reviews part of the concatenation of causes that resulted in World War II in the Pacific. It is undertaken in memory of Alice and all those who served there, who died there, or who came home from their service with disease and scars.

Morison begins his *The Rising Sun in the Pacific* with a quote from Saint James: "Ye lust and have not; ye kill and desire to have." There was lust enough on all sides in the years of empire-building and expansion that led to war in the Pacific—lust for power, lust for markets cornered, lust for wealth and resources, the lust of nations, and the lust of corporations. Such desires mixed with and drew from a plethora of ideologies, agendas, and rationalizations.

It was the era of colonialism, when nations sought their day in the sun, built high-seas fleets, and contested for dominions and destinies. Great Britain, the envy of all imperialists, along with Spain, the Netherlands, and France, had established their claims in the Pacific before the United States acquired, by war with Spain, the Philippines, and Guam. Even where there was no initial intention of conquest, there was a built-in escalation of involvement. Intention for trade led to the conviction that if the trader from the outside was to take over all aspects of the source of trade, the business would be done more efficiently, and the results would be better for everyone. After all, wasn't this the manifest duty of higher and more efficient civilizations?

When Alice reached Manila in the fall of 1941, colonialism still played an important role. Figuratively, colonialism spread a white linen tea cloth over the very ugly conceptions of ethnocentrism. Ethnocentrism in the Pacific, in turn, was linked with three other

-isms, all malignant in their own way: ultranationalism, an Asian version of fascism, and totalitarianism.

At the same time Western industrialization was seeking new resources and creating the need for additional markets, technology, like a great fire, was creating its own wind, and making the old strategies and weapons obsolete.

In 1905, eleven years before Alice was born, a naval engagement was fought in the Tsushima Strait (located between Japan and the Korean Peninsula), in which the Imperial Navy of Japan, with its superior technology, devastated a large part of the Russian fleet. Japan had emerged from a technologically backward and secluded entity to a modern sea power capable of defeating a Western navy. Many American leaders looked forward to having Japan as an agreeable and capable ally.

Although a latecomer among the national expansionists in the Pacific, the United States had been influential in the Far East for years. There was a special association with Japan, which began in 1853 when Commodore Matthew Perry anchored four naval vessels in Edo Bay (present-day Tokyo) and sought trade agreements. The impact of Perry's appearances, along with changes afoot in Japan's inner circle, led to a "treaty of trade and friendship" between the Japanese and the Americans. The port of Nagasaki was opened, diplomatic representation was granted, and resident rights were given to Americans.

At the signing of the treaty, American diplomats presented token gifts to the emperor as symbols of a new age, including a miniature train and a telegraph instrument. It was a little like Christmas, and the significance of the telegraph and the train was not lost on the recipients. As Robert Bridges was to write, the Japanese would see "the electric light [in] the West, and come to worship."[2]

The Japanese feudal government that Perry had dealt with was replaced by the Meiji Restoration ("Meiji" meaning "enlightened rule"). Although the result was an oligarchy rather than a democracy, American diplomats were optimistic. When Alice was born in 1916, Japan and the United States were allies. Many Americans, including Theodore Roosevelt, considered Japan the new, hardworking, and useful kid on the block, a source of trade, a refueling opportunity for the U.S. fleet, and a block to any future Russian expansion.

Building an alliance with Japan was a dangerous game, for Japan was increasingly interested in its own colonization and expansion. The country was busy annexing Formosa (present-day Taiwan) and Korea, while aggressively making demands on China. Any American business-man could understand Japan's desire to be a modern power, yet, despite all the bowing, handshaking, and diplomatic agreements between the United States and Japan, there remained a disconnect—a fundamental difference in worldviews, cultural backgrounds, and physical needs.

—*∿*—

In contrast, daily life in Brownville continued much the same, the hum-drum sprinkled with little excitements. The weather in August 1922 had been accommodating for the Radcliffe Chautauqua concerts. In the fall, one of the wealthier families who owned a big house turned the attic into a Halloween delight, with orange pumpkins and electrically illumi-nated witches. There were joys, concerns, and cautionary notes. Typical of the latter, the Central Maine Power Company filled half a page in the county newspaper with a cartoon wake-up call: Maine needed to develop her resources, because money and young people were leaving for better opportunities.

—*∿*—

On the international scene, naval limitation acts and conferences sought to maintain the interest of the larger powers, while eliminating costly naval arms races and keeping the peace. At the Washington Disarma-ment Conference held in 1921–1922, major powers including Japan agreed to ratios fixing the number of ships in their fleets. It was agreed "to respect each other in the Pacific" and to consult each other in the event of any aggressive action. Nine world powers (including Japan) agreed to open trade with China and to guarantee that country's independence and territorial integrity.

Of special interest to this biography was the allowance by treaty of defensive endeavors. As a result, the United States began the construction in 1922 of the Malinta Tunnel on Corregidor. The blasting of this defensive structure within a mountain would take ten years.[3]

Eight years after the disarmament conference in Washington, the London Naval Conference was convened. More ship ratios were set, and more scrapping of capital ships was agreed upon. Japan, following its own agenda, rebuilt one of her battleships—still under construction, and by treaty scheduled to be scrapped—into her first heavy-class aircraft carrier.

Although Japan outwardly agreed to these treaties and agreements, her aristocratic militarists saw the treaties as a means of keeping Japan subservient. In reaction, they espoused the tradition of *bushido*, the way of the warrior. Their spirit of aggressive nationalism and their call for expansionism steadily gained predominance. Their takeover of Japan was postponed only by the devastation of the Tokyo earthquake in 1923.[4]

Among the ideologies fueling political and military fervor in Japan was the *Kodo-ha* (the Imperial Way faction). This movement was strongest among lower- and middle-class military officers. It expressed hatred for the growing influence of rich white men and the industrialization they had fostered. The movement advocated a military takeover of the government and a return to aggressive action abroad.

Despite the rallies of more peaceful and liberal views, a powerful mixing of an old feudal and warrior ethos with an emerging fascism was building momentum. Increasingly, any opposition to the emerging militarism and imperialism was silenced with police powers derived, ironically, from the Peace Preservation Law (1925), passed to quell civil violence.

Into this formation of Imperial Japan came worldwide Depression and the collapse of the silk market, so important to the Japanese economy. In December of 1926, Emperor Hirohito assumed the throne amid revolt and political turmoil. The military answer to the nation's economic and social distress was the occupation of China. The era of *Showa* had begun for Japan, the era euphemistically called "enlightened peace."

—◦◦◦—

Brownville, Maine, 1931: A crowd of Brownville residents went to a traveling carnival that had set up in a field in Milo. Catherine Zwicker, Alice's older sister, went with her mother to Waterville to visit an aunt. From there, she continued on to Gorham Normal School near Portland, Maine, where she would train to be a teacher. Alice was thoroughly enjoying her junior year in Brownville High School.

—◦◦◦—

In that same year, 1931, an "alleged bomb" on the South Manchurian Railway gave the Japanese army an excuse to invade Manchuria. Japan was once again at war with China. This time, years of military preparation, mental conditioning, and technological advance were to reveal a fearsome and terrible efficiency.

In Japan, there rose out of the country's past a concept that gave a new and powerful justification for expansionism and manifest destiny: *Hakko Ichiu*—"bringing the eight corners of the world under one roof." Whatever the original significance of this phrase, its new intent was to create, under Japan's divine emperor, an Asian—even a worldwide— hegemony characterized by peace and prosperity. This concept was given a resounding appellation: the Greater East Asia Co-Prosperity Sphere. With increased solidarity, Japanese industrialists, influenced by the possibility of extended markets and profits, joined with the militarists, and the winds of "divine mission" were about to blow their hot breath of destruction across the Far East.

In 1936, Japan withdrew from the Naval Treaty and began an extensive program of naval construction. By 1941, her fleet would be more powerful than the Allied fleet that could be assembled to oppose her in the Pacific. And then, with a contrived incident at the Marco Polo Bridge near Peking (1937), the Imperial Army of Japan swept into China itself, where U.S. patrol boats steamed on the Yangtze River, protecting American corporate interests, American citizens, and a united commerce.[5] There would be four more years of diplomatic efforts, but in China there would be no peace, and senior U.S. naval officers were sure that the next war would be fought with the Empire of Japan.

———

Bangor, 1937: The eagles turned above the Penobscot salmon pool, while at the hospital on the high riverbank, Alice was nearing the end of her passage toward becoming a registered nurse.

4

BECOMING A LADY WITH A LAMP

On a Sunday afternoon in early September 1934, Alice, her parents, and her sister Helena rode to Bangor with neighbor Grace Foulkes and her daughter Margaret. They all had visiting to do, and when that was done, they left Alice at the hospital dormitory to begin the fulfillment of her lifelong dream, her training as a nurse.

Alice was eighteen years old and found her new venture at Eastern Maine General Hospital to be exciting and scary at the same time. The three stories of the brick student nurses' dormitory (four stories, if one counted the dormer-windowed attic) did not look like Brownville, nor did it feel like home. The busy hospital was far different from the world she had known. She was homesick at times that first year. Her second year was much better, when her sister Helena joined her as a student nurse.

It seemed like a decade since she had graduated from high school. She had kept busy during the year she had waited to enter her nurses' training program. She and Helena, along with a group of their chums, were in a pageant called *Down in the Garden.* During Brownville's an-nual Old Home Celebration, she had performed as a maid in what the county newspaper acclaimed as a "most successful play." Then members of her high school class, along with members of the church choir, had surprised her with a birthday party, followed by a dance. Despite all the excitement, the summer before the start of training had dragged.

There was a solid respect for nursing in Brownville and Milo. During the great flu epidemic of 1918, six nurses from these small towns had volunteered to go to Camp Devens in Massachusetts, where nearly nine thousand servicemen were desperately sick. Such a response to hazardous duty was extraordinary. It must have involved nearly every nurse those two towns had to offer.[1]

In this respectful environment, the call to nursing came early to Alice.

There are very few photographs of Alice in which she is not laughing, or at least displaying her delightful smile; however, one photo displays no silliness whatsoever. The photo was taken when Alice was perhaps five. She is wearing a white frock, and someone has fashioned a wraparound nurse's cap with a large red cross placed squarely in the front. Her hands are held in serious intent, and her expression signifies that she means business.

In the fall of 1934, as Alice settled into her dormitory room, that calling became reality, one characterized by hard work and a growing sense of responsibility.

Eastern Maine General Hospital (EMGH) was a citadel of healing located on the banks of the dark-flowing Penobscot River. It had been founded with distinguished medical and historical associations. The drawing up of incorporation papers was held in one of the large tall-posted Bangor homes, where Dr. Elliott Carr Cutler, an outstanding figure at Harvard Medical School and a leader in American surgical practice, had been born. In addition, the president of the new hospital cooperation was General Charles Hamlin, son of Hannibal Hamlin, who had served as Lincoln's vice president. The hospital's first superintendent was the redoubtable Elizabeth Spratt, a graduate of Boston City Hospital's School of Nursing (later, part of the Boston Medical Center).

As a general hospital, the new facility in Bangor served two-thirds of the state's geography and one-third of its population. During Alice's years there as a student nurse, EMGH had been approved by the American College of Surgeons. It was a busy place, operating at capacity, concerned with overcrowding, and treating four thousand patients annually in an era when a patient's average hospital stay was thirteen days.

The creation of the hospital had been quickly followed by the establishment of a program for training nurses. This program became accredited by the states of Maine and New York. Graduates were certified to practice in both states, a fact that Alice and many other nurses trained there would find advantageous.

From the start, the hospital directors resolved that no patient would be turned away because of an inability to pay for treatment. It was a commendable decision; however, this intention contributed to a precarious balance of income and operational expenditures. Under these conditions, student nurses became an essential element of hospital staffing. There was a symbiotic relationship between the hospital and its matriculating nurses. Although these young women were not paid for the hours they worked on the wards, their tuition for the nursing program was only two hundred dollars per year, which explains how the Zwickers could afford to send Alice to nursing school and, a year later, to have two of their daughters enrolled in the program at the same time.

The many hours that student nurses spent on duty was the subject of debate. In 1937, the year Alice graduated, the report of the New York State Board of Nurse Education's accreditation team was particularly concerned with the schedule for student nurses, especially when they were on night duty. They worked from 9:00 p.m. to 7:00 a.m., seven nights a week, for six-week stints. That added up to seventy hours a week, "exclusive of classes and preparation for classes."

Just as critical was the question of the quality of instruction. Head nurses, hard-pressed to complete their everyday tasks—which at times included acting as admitting nurses for incoming patients—were also expected to instruct the students. In many cases, it was difficult to see how sufficient teaching could get accomplished, given their heavy workload. In one case, visiting observers found a student nurse acting in the capacity of head nurse. That incident got everyone's attention.

No existing nursing program at the time would have properly prepared Alice and her colleagues for the ordeal of handling triage amid the carnage and horrendous conditions they would face during the war; however, they were taught to work hard, to take responsibility, and to improvise under difficult conditions, in a wide range of medical situations. As important as any preparation they received was their drilling in hygiene and in confining infectious disease.

Despite the economics and the patient loads, the aim of the nursing school administration at EMGH was to graduate medically educated nurses. Such a goal necessitated demanding coursework. In Alice's last year of training, the nursing program at EMGH was negotiating an affiliation with the University of Maine, but for Alice and the other seventy-five student nurses then in the program, the required nine hundred hours of classroom instruction was provided by the hospital staff. The hours per subject varied widely: 209 hours for nursing arts (including hygiene and sanitation), 112 hours in anatomy and physiology, forty-five hours in surgical nursing, fifteen hours in diet therapy, and eight hours in consideration of what was listed as "sociology-pathology." Alice did best in chemistry, earning a grade of ninety-three. She got an eighty-seven in pharmacology, and an eighty-five in surgical nursing.

Survival in the program demanded mental ability, physical capability, and, above all, determination. The medical profession, impressed with the rigorous demands of its own practice, always seems intent on an early winnowing-out process of its potential personnel. Not all who enrolled at EMGH finished the program, or even completed the first year. In the year that Alice was a senior, the administration was encouraged when only twelve students dropped out.

Discipline was strict. Conduct in the nurses' residence was stipulated in seventy-four "do's and don'ts." Nurses were not to sweep dirt from their rooms into the corridors. Their beds were not to be left unmade. They were to use twenty-five-watt lightbulbs in their rooms; they "were not to call out of the windows to anyone"; and no radios were to be used between 8:00 a.m. and 3:30 p.m. The rule on radio playing wasn't too restrictive. The programs Alice and her friends looked forward to the most came on in the evening, and included those that featured beauty tips or the sounds of Wayne King's or Guy Lombardo's orchestras playing "Cocktails for Two," "Riptide," "Best of My Heart," or "You're My Lucky Charm"—music that urged the listener to transform the tune into motion on a dance floor.

There was another set of rules that pertained to personal and professional conduct in general. Nurses were not to leave the dormitory with coats over their uniforms. Fortunately there was a covered passage from the nurses' quarters to the hospital. They were not to visit wards when not on duty. They could use the kitchen and the sewing room. Students were to be in their rooms by 10:30 p.m. unless on night duty. They were allowed to be out late (returning by midnight) eight nights per month. Nursing students were required to sign out each time they "left the hill" (hospital grounds). Finally, students were requested "to select social contacts wisely."

The nurses' residence, built eight years before Alice began training, was described as having "everything necessary to the comfort of the residents." But while there was running water in every room, overcrowding was a problem in Alice's day, with some students being forced to live in the attic area. They were not charged for room and board. The nurses ate the hospital fare, which evidently was adequate. However, Alice often went to bed thinking about the sandwiches sitting in the display case at The Coffee Pot, a sandwich shop just down the street from the hospital. She and her sister went there on many Saturday evenings.

If the nursing student's life sounds spartan, it was not so very different from what many of them were used to at home. Still, the young women came up with ingenious ways to inject fun and excitement into their routine. There were special functions, like a Halloween masque, a party at Christmas, a dance at graduation time, and the chance to get home for visits.

Occasionally, Alice's parents came to Bangor by train to visit their two daughters in training, and Alice got back to Brownville and the house on Pleasant Street more often as time went on. When engaging young Dr. Edward Savage drove Alice to Brownville, it might have been only for a few hours, but it was still worth the trip. Not so many years later, when Alice was a prisoner of the Japanese, she made a list of people she wanted to remember, and Dr. Savage was on it.

In 1936, she was home for a whole week at Thanksgiving time. It rained a lot during that vacation, but it was still precious time together. The family kaleidoscope was turning. Older sister Catherine was becoming upwardly mobile. She taught school and boarded in a neighboring town, but she now owned a 1933 Plymouth coupe, so could get home whenever she wanted. Brothers Ken and Eli were full of town gossip and school news. Alice's youngest sister, Geraldine, was taking her turn keeping up the family reputation, having just made the high school honor roll.

Sometimes Alice brought with her a close friend, fellow nursing student Bertha Grant from Easton, Maine. Bertha fitted in well. She was nimble on the ukulele, and Alice's youngest brother Eli thought she was very attractive.

Important to Alice's professional development were the seventy days spent training in the operating room. She had other clinical experiences that would be of special relevance, including thirty days of tuberculosis nursing.

In her third year of training, the horizons of Alice's world sprang outward again with two rotations in Boston. The nursing program at Eastern Maine had a long-standing arrangement that allowed its student nurses to work at Boston Children's Hospital for some ninety days, along with another tour of duty in obstetrics at the Boston Lying-In Hospital. While the latter sounds resoundingly Victorian, Boston Lying-In was founded five years before Victoria became queen. Now merged with the Harvard-affiliated Peter Bent Brigham Hospital, Boston Lying-In had trained many thousands of nurses before Alice arrived. It was an exacting experience, but, as Alice wrote home, the student nurses from Bangor were treated well and enjoyed good accommodations in the nurses' quarters.

Children's Hospital was both a joy and a difficult experience for Alice. Although it was terrible to see little ones so pitifully sick, Alice had a special way with children. Later, she developed close relationships with her nephews and nieces, who loved her not simply because she gave the best Christmas presents but because life had a special fascination when they were with their Aunt Alice. She never seemed to tire of reading to them, and she could always think of fun things to do or places to go. One Christmas when Aunt Alice was away at war and no one in the family knew whether she was alive or dead, sister Helena asked her little boy what he wanted Santa Claus to bring him. He answered, "Just to bring Aunt Alice home."

It was at Children's Hospital that Alice met and became fast friends with nursing student Ann Dunleavy. When Ann later married Frank McAlevey, the three remained close. That friendship was to play an important role in Alice's later life.

Boston Lying-In Hospital had a distinguished history, pioneering in the reduction of deaths from infection and in the employment of antiseptic conditions, but it was while she was training there that Alice got a strep infection. Of course, she could have contracted the germs at the movies or a coffee shop. The results were serious: Alice was diagnosed with rheumatic fever. Antibiotics have made this ailment rare in developed countries these days; however, it remains an involved disease in which the bacterium tricks the body's immune system into attacking its own tissue—especially that of the heart, joints, and central nervous system. In the 1930s, bed rest was the prescribed treatment.

Alice's rest treatment brought her back to Brownville. Her recovery progressed rapidly enough for her to do some private practice before she returned to Eastern Maine General to complete her training program. One of her patients was a rather controversial, well-off, part-time resident of Brownville. It was good experience. A nurse has to get along with all kinds of people, and Alice found she could handle the most difficult of patients along with the easiest.

"Answering a calling" is a splendid old phrase, and nursing is definitely a calling—something you must appreciate if you are to fully understand what Alice and the army nurses experienced in the Philippines during World War II. Early on in their training experience, the capping ceremony provided a symbolic as well as tangible expression of this vocation.

At Eastern Maine General, as in many other training programs, the capping ceremony was accompanied by the lighting of the Nightingale lamps, which each young woman carried and ignited at a central flame. The nursing students at Bangor did not have to look far for an example of a woman pioneer in the art of nursing. Dorothea Dix, who was appointed the superintendent of nurses during the Civil War, was born in the adjacent town of Hampden, Maine.

But it was not simply the inspiration from the past that made the difference; there also had to be an inner core of compassion—an ethic of caring, to use Nel Noddings's phrase—which was part of what each young woman brought with her. It was a deep commitment reinforced by her three years of training. Lives would be entrusted to her care. There was a "voice" that seemed to announce, "This calling to nursing is not about you; it is about them."[2]

Alice was one of eighteen nurses who graduated from Eastern Maine General School of Nursing in 1937. Her grades had been respectable. Her average grade was an eighty-five, which she earned in medical and surgical emergencies, advanced nursing, pathology, surgical lectures, and public health. She still had coursework to finish due to her episode with rheumatic fever. Her diploma would be dated April 1938, but she would participate fully in graduation with her class. The address was given by Elizabeth Sullivan, supervisor of Schools of Nursing in the Commonwealth of Massachusetts. A. Stanley Cayting, violin virtuoso of the Northern Conservatory of Music, played two solos, and, much to Alice's excitement, there was a reception and a dance.

Their class song had a stanza that was more meaningful than perhaps anyone realized at the time:

> We came from many places,
> We shall go to many more,
> But where'er our journey takes us,
> May we take thy nursing lore.

The Depression persisted after Alice's graduation. Private-duty nurses were getting two dollars per day, which was better than the pay for hospital duty. Hospitals depended more on student nurses, and positions were hard to find. Having become a registered nurse, Alice did general nursing at the small private hospital in Milo, Maine, which Eleanor McNaughton, a New England Deaconess nurse, had opened.[3] She also nursed at Mayo Hospital in Dover-Foxcroft until April of 1940, when a position as charge nurse opened at the Eastern Maine General Hospital. Seven months later, Alice was a head surgical nurse at her alma mater.

The job came with a great deal of responsibility, and was much busier than one might expect. The surgical staff routinely worked three to four hours overtime on a daily basis. In addition to assisting in operations, surgical nurses were also required to prepare saline solutions for irrigation, fold surgical sponges, store all surgical supplies, wash and sterilize instruments, assemble surgical trays, wrap sutures on reels, transport patients, and clean the operating room. Dust and flies were constant problems until the advent of air-conditioning systems.

Nonetheless, it was challenging, interesting, even exciting work. Alice had found a professional specialty in the operating room.

5

WAFTING OF GARDENIA
AND THE ERUPTION OF WAR

The United States drew closer to World War II with fewer than a thousand nurses in the Army Nurse Corps.[1] Although there were many people who thought that to be prepared for war was to make the next conflict inevitable, others were concerned about America's lack of readiness. Military planners estimated that the existing number of nurses would have to be increased more than fifty times should another world war take place.

The Red Cross, which led the recruitment of military nurses, mounted a campaign epitomized in posters featuring wonderful young women wearing white caps, with the edges of their blue capes turned back to show the red lining. There were notices in nursing magazines and newspapers that emphasized the advantages of more pay, the opportunity to serve one's country, and the chance for advancement and adventure. Beyond such inducements there was the chance that a new army nurse might, by the luck of the draw, be assigned to the plum of romantic assignments—the subtropical paradise of Manila in the Philippines.

Alice had much to think about as she looked out the window of her room onto Bangor's State Street. During the grubby remnants of the winter of 1940–1941, the cold shadows of the Great Depression still lingered. Although graphs might have depicted an encouraging rise in the national per-person income, the unemployment figure was still at 15 percent.

Alice had enjoyed her time on the hospital staff, especially instructing nursing students in the operating room and on the wards, but she was closer to twenty-four than twenty-three. The year before she had been a bridesmaid at her sister Catherine's wedding, and that was a wake-up call. It was time to think about a long-term career or finding that right man. It was also time to do something really exciting, even daring, before it was too late.

Across the nation, other young nurses were also considering their futures.

Mildred Dalton, who was to become one of Alice's dearest friends, graduated third in her class from the training program at Grady Hospital in Atlanta, and was made head nurse on the surgical ward of the same hospital. Many years later, at age ninety-seven, Mildred remembered:

> I stayed two years and, looking around me, decided that was as far as I would get without going to college, and I didn't have money for that. I had friends in the Army at Fort McPherson in Atlanta, and visiting them heard all the stories of working half days, traveling all over the world, [and having] a month vacation, and [I] said, "That's for me."[2]

Alice had similar thoughts. Like many nurses contemplating serving in the army, Alice wanted to make enough money to send some home. Although army nurses earned only half the salary of their male counterparts in the service, they were making more than Alice could earn in a hospital, or in private practice. Then there was the matter of the provided board and keep, not to mention job security.

All of these were down-to-earth considerations, but there was another tug—something calling from beyond Bangor's State Street, beckoning toward a new sense of personal freedom.

And what if one was lucky enough to be posted to a place like the Philippines? Alice had heard the seductive descriptions: the sun-warmed beaches and the moonlit, gardenia-scented nights. Years later, historian Elizabeth Norman would capture the possibilities when she wrote that a nurse's wardrobe in the Philippines need only include "a uniform, a bathing suit, and an evening gown."[3]

By March 1941, Alice had decided to join the Army Nurse Corps. She took the oath on the fourth of March in Bangor—not quite the Ides of March, but close enough. There was no one to tell her that the far Pacific might soon become a very dangerous place. At that time, and for months to come, not even General Douglas MacArthur knew that government officials at the highest U.S. and British echelons had agreed that, when the United States came into the war, it would be the European theater, not the Pacific, that would receive first attention. For those stationed in the Philippines, encircled as it was by islands occupied by the Japanese, this decision would have disastrous consequences.

On April 21, 1941, Alice reported to Camp Edwards on Cape Cod. The base was rapidly expanding. During the previous October, the draft had been reinstated, and Edwards had become a training center in the army's new program of mobilization. Accommodations for thirty thousand soldiers had been built at Edwards in four months. A year after Alice's arrival, a field training school was instituted at Edwards that would prepare 2,500 nurses, but there was no such preparation available in the spring of 1941. Although an army medical field school had been introduced as early as 1921, the prevailing wisdom was that the general training provided to nurses in civilian hospitals would be sufficient for military service.

Alice received the customary battery of shots and vaccinations, including smallpox, typhoid, and cholera immunizations. She was assigned duty at the base hospital, got fingerprinted, and received her beneficiary card. She was confined to the barracks for three days with an "intestinal upset," but still Alice decided that "the Army was O.K."

On Wednesday, June 25, Alice arrived home for a week's furlough. Her admirer from Eastern Maine General, Dr. Edward Savage, met the train at Bangor and drove her on the last lap of her journey to Brownville. He stayed overnight as a guest. Then members of the family gathered, including Helena and her husband; Geraldine; and another couple, James Nason and his wife, Ellen Cushing, who had trained in Bangor with Alice and Helena.

It was wonderful and exhilarating to be home—so much like old times! On Friday, there was a crashing thundershower that disrupted the power, but not the ongoing party. Alice would return to duty before Old Home Week took place, but plans for this annual event were well known and already being discussed. As an added bit of excitement, Hunt's three-ring circus, with trained animals and "one hundred new acts," was in Dover-Foxcroft.

Alice would be home once more before she left for overseas. It was a flying visit. She had applied for two years of duty in the Philippines, made the list of those going, and was set to sail shortly. Alice's youngest brother, Eli, was at a school dance when Alice appeared in the auditorium. She kissed him and said good-bye.

The grand adventure began when the train left the railroad station at Buzzards Bay, Cape Cod. With Alice were nurses Letha McHale, Catherine Acorn, Anne Wurtz, Helen Cassiani, and Rita Palmer. These young women would become bound together in a special comradeship born in travail of which they had no inkling at the time.

Alice had never been beyond Boston. Disappointingly, there was not much time for shopping in San Francisco. The nurses had orders to report to the U.S. Army Transport *Willard A. Holbrook*, which was loading for the Philippines. Perhaps none of the nurses who boarded the *Holbrook* in October of 1941 was aware that the ship had recently been involved in evacuating military dependents from the Philippines.

The vessel was a gray shadow of the passenger ship she had been when she had carried the colors of the American President Lines and participated in the rich Asian trade. She had been the *President Taft* then. Some of the nurses thought the ship was an ugly color, but she was large, in some ways commodious (at least by army standards), and filled with handsome young men of the 19th Bombardment Group. Nothing was going to tarnish this adventure.

Aboard were other army nurses: Eleanor Garen from Indiana, Phyllis Arnold from Minnesota, Imogene (Jeanne) Kennedy from Mississippi, Millie Dalton and Grace Hallman from Georgia, and Leona Gastinger, who hailed from Alabama. Seven months later, Leona would be somewhere in the outer blackness of Manila Bay, transferring to the submarine *Spearfish*, while the majority of nurses would remain in a tunnel on shell-ripped Corregidor, awaiting the inevitable arrival of the Japanese.

The *Holbrook* left harbor with the evening tide and that night ran into rough weather that set her rolling. Off and on, and mostly on, it was seasick-ish weather all the way to Hawaii. The troops were not allowed shore leave at Honolulu, but the nurses were able to visit the city. For Alice the vaunted paradise of the Pacific Islands had not been exaggerated. She made up her mind that she had to live in Hawaii someday, except at Christmas. There had to be snow for Christmas.

The weather improved as they left Hawaii for Manila. The *Holbrook* picked up the company of two four-stacked destroyers, one on each side. Later, Phyllis Arnold was a little hard on herself for not fully realizing the implication:

> The closer we got to the Philippines, [the more] I should have realized how serious it was, but at the time I was a very slap-happy person. I loved to dance, I enjoyed being a good nurse, but when I was off duty, I either danced, played golf [or] tennis, or went swimming.[4]

If Alice had any second thoughts, the sight of those two destroyers plowing the Pacific water into white curls took away any qualms. Suppose Japan *did* try something; what would its chances be against the United States? Japan was no bigger than California.

As the *Holbrook* neared the International Date Line, Alice and her nurse companions received a summons from King Neptune, "Ruler of the Raging Main." On October 12, along with the other "pollywogs," Alice was conducted in her bathing suit before the long-bearded king and his court seated on the deck, surrounded by a vocal crowd of sailors. With much water, a modicum of embarrassment, and a lot of ceremony, the nurses became "Sir Shellbacks," members of the Ancient Order of the Deep. The initiation was hard duty for the ship's officers and seamen, but somebody had to do it.

The harbor at Guam had been mined, but again, the nurses went ashore by launch. There was no mistaking the adventure and the romance. By then, Alice was fully enthralled by islands that "wave their fronded palms in air." She would write of her voyage to the Philippines: "Many incidents to say the least! Never a dull moment on *that* cruise!!"[5]

The *Holbrook* docked at Pier Seven in Manila on October 23, 1941. A band in white uniform was stirring the warm air with a march, and the nurses came down the gangplank wearing their best dresses and high heels. The "cruise" had taken nineteen days; the last half, after the storms, had been wonderful.

During 1941, the band had been called to play at an increasing number of "boat days," as the ship dockings were called. Had Alice arrived two weeks earlier, she could have witnessed the arrival of the convoy escorted by the battleship *Arizona.* The *President Coolidge,* which was part of that convoy, carried the new Stuart tanks of the 194th Tank Battalion. When they were unloaded, the battalion had rolled past General MacArthur in review. It was a great show, and comforting, if any comfort was sought.

In the spring of 1941, when fighting the Japanese seemed inevitable to a growing number in the military, General Jonathan Wainwright had commented that the "sparkle" had gone out of Manila. But if it had, Alice was unaware of the loss. There were cars waiting to take the nurses to the Army and Navy Club to enjoy the traditional libation of gin, and then on to Sternberg General Hospital, where the nurses were to report.

The route they took to Sternberg General was short and scenic, skirting the old walled city—the "Intramuros," built by the Spanish in 1641. All of this antiquity was now surrounded by the rush of downtown

Manila, awash with activity. Everywhere there was something to see. Sternberg was an island of shaded porticoes, an "alabaster quadrangle," as Elizabeth Norman describes it, where the nursing quarters featured "Elysian rooms . . . [with] wicker furniture . . . and mahogany ceiling fans gently turning the tropical air."[6]

It was from Sternberg that Captain Maude Davison commanded the Army Nurse Corps in the Philippines. Captain Davison had joined the Corps in 1918, when the United States was fighting a world war "to make the world safe for democracy." She nursed through the horrors of the great flu epidemic, and also worked in famine-stricken Germany. She was a career professional, a graduate of Columbia, strict and capable of thinking for herself when things got tough. The new nurses thought her cold, and most would not change that judgment, but they would come to realize how much they owed her.

Captain Davison and her second in command, Lieutenant Josie Nesbit, decided where the incoming nurses were to be stationed—not so much by where they were needed at the present time as by where they would be required if trouble erupted. On October 30, Maude Davison ordered Alice to Fort William McKinley, seven miles south of Manila.

Alice's week at Sternberg was long enough to receive the usual immunizations. She became somewhat acclimated to the heat and humidity, discovered the blessing of ceiling fans, and learned that one kept a light burning in one's closet to discourage the damp and mildew.

She also became aware of certain facts about the city: One did not eat indiscriminately when abroad in Manila. Some eateries, the nurses were told, may have looked respectable from the street, but washed dishes in filthy streams behind their establishments. That story was graphic enough to emphasize the dangers of contamination. There were also sober warnings about venereal disease and tuberculosis, both of which were prevalent in the Philippines. Last, but not to be taken lightly, were areas in the city where the nurses were told not to go, whether they were escorted or not. Despite such warnings, Manila was where the "action" was, and Alice may have been disappointed to be stationed outside the main city.

Fort McKinley, however, was not a bad alternative. It was neither isolated nor limited in opportunities. It was a large establishment—some 152 acres—large enough to have trolley service to the post pool and to its own bowling alley, movie theater, and golf course. The base had its own unique history, as well. It was established during the Philippine-American War when, in true colonial fashion, the United States had put down an attempt of Filipino rebels to gain freedom. (There was nothing about the squelching of this uprising in the history book that Alice had studied.)

In the fall of 1941, there were new threats and concerns, and Fort McKinley's purpose represented the combined interests of the United States and the Philippines. It was the home of the 57th Infantry Regiment of Philippine Scouts, the best of the Filipino troops, and the headquarters of MacArthur's U.S. Armed Forces Far East.

When Alice joined the nursing staff at Fort McKinley, the independence that the rebels had sought at the turn of the century was finally being actualized. Still, the easy life of colonialism lingered. Under the shade of the acacia trees, three to four nurses were housed in each bungalow, each in her own room with a shared bath, dining facilities, and a screened-in porch with a swing. Alice thought the setup was pretty "nifty." At the street end of each bungalow walk, the nurses had their names displayed on white boards—handy for someone who was picking one of them up. Houseboys did the laundry and the errands; Filipino servants brought fresh-squeezed fruit juice in the morning, and kept the floors polished by "skating" around with coconut shells strapped to their feet.

Alice's two bungalow mates were lieutenants Frankie Lewey and Minnie Breese. Frankie was from Texas, and Minnie from Illinois. They were older than Alice but full of fun. Minnie had been at McKinley a month before Alice arrived, and her experience came in handy.

Nurses fresh from stateside hospitals found some of the medical equipment primitive. Phyllis Arnold told Alice that the ambulances must have come from the Spanish-American War. Although there was some catching up to do, what had been a dispensary for the Philippine

Scouts was rapidly becoming a proficient 250-bed facility. Behind all this activity, there seemed to be a sense of urgency, whatever that meant.

Alice heard the rumors. Pilots who dated the nurses told of increased meetings with flights of Japanese aircraft, while soldiers and sailors came and went on patrols and exercises with greater frequency. In the nurses' mess, Chief Nurse Eleanor O'Neal would joke, "Have another biscuit, girls. You're going to need this when the Japs get us."[7] The nurses would laugh. They all knew that the real war was in Europe and half a world away.

It was hard to imagine war, anyway. There was so much time, and so many fun activities with which to fill it. Because so many American families—except those of the civilian business community—had been sent back to the States, the number of patients was reduced. Nurses on day duty worked four-hour shifts, which was long enough in the heat. Those on nights worked eight-hour shifts, but they were young, and often headed out to the golf course or the crescents of ocean beach when they got off duty. In the softer warmth of evening, there were parties at the Officers' Club, with the men happy to display their culinary accomplishments at the barbecue.

There were glorious evenings when couples went into Manila to drive Dewey Boulevard and be spellbound by the sunsets. Alice saw a sunset there that she never forgot. Years later, she told an audience, "I saw many unpleasant things, but I also saw a sunset across that China Sea that was worth writing home about."[8] Sunsets and sunrises were to become redeeming moments during the challenging times ahead.

And then, when the evening stars came out, couples might turn to dancing under the light-spangled ceilings at the Manila Hotel, the La Paloma Club, or the exclusive haven of the Army and Navy Club, set, as it was, by the sea on three acres of palms and flame trees rising amid the red and purple splashes of bougainvillea. Upon arriving in Manila, Alice received a guest card extending her privileges to the Army and Navy Club, free of charge, good for fifteen days. She wondered how she could afford to pay for membership and still send money home.

Of Manila before the war Alice wrote: "Great spot! What night life! I loved it!!"[9] If only her mother, who loved flowers, could have seen the blooms. The Reverend Mr. Loudon of the Brownville Congregational Church had never described heaven as being so delectable. It seemed there was music and dancing everywhere. The music came from both the place and the people, and rang with converging traditions.

The La Paloma Club, for instance, was named for a Spanish song. Originally the tune was inspired by an ancient Greek legend in which white doves were said to be the spirits of drowned sailors finally coming home.

Dance clubs were not the only choices. Right in the middle of the old Spanish architecture along Taft Avenue was the rounded glass Art Deco front of the Jai Alai, an arena for an old Basque game akin to handball, which had become a leading sport and occasion for gambling in the Philippines. The Jai Alai had exotic food, dancing, and entertainment. It was all new to Alice, and she reveled in the rich experiences Manila offered.

She had also found a friend of interest. His name was Robert "Bob" Dameron, a thirty-five-year-old divorcé and district manager for the Southern California Fruit Exchange, Sunkist. He resembled Joe DiMaggio, and was half a head taller than Alice when she was wearing heels. He was a fun-loving guy, and they made an attractive couple.[10]

She had also met Fred Rising Newell Jr., a twenty-five-year-old Annapolis graduate. A New Englander, Fred was born on Chestnut Hill in Brattleboro, Vermont, and was handsome in an all-American way. When Alice met him, he was on shore duty with the naval police.

Mildred Dalton Manning, Alice's dear friend, remembered that Alice always had admirers. She "was very attractive, and a warm person."[11] But from almost the very first, Alice knew that Fred was the man she wanted to marry. He presented her with a formal photograph of himself taken in his dress whites. He also gave her a photo of his parents, Dr. and Mrs. Newell. That photo was almost like an engagement ring.

The grand New Year's Gala was fast approaching, but with the Christmas season came increased thoughts of home. Alice sent a Christmas card to her father: "Gifts will come later," she wrote, "probably after New Year's, when there won't be such a rush." There would be snow on the mountains, if not on the lawns, of Brownville. The branches of the hardwood trees along the river would become a white lace of frost, and families would soon be searching for just the right Christmas tree.

She did not know that her parents were writing letters to her—words from home that she would not read until three harrowing years had passed. In one of his long epistles, her father jokingly observed that when all of these letters reached her, she would have to take a week off to read them. He was working again in Portland on outside carpentry jobs, which was cold on the fingers. He had celebrated his birthday and received eight cards; Alice's mother had come down from home with a birthday cake and a new pair of heavy pants as a gift. The pants were too long, but Mary had brought needle and thread along. "She doesn't miss very much, does she?" Alice's dad added. Helena's son, Dennis, was growing to beat the band, and could laugh out loud. Eli, Alice's youngest brother, also kept growing, and could no longer wear Ken's clothes. It was all news from home that Alice would have relished.

She sent a telegram to her sister Catherine, who was married and living in Derby, Maine, Milo's companion community. Western Union had supplied the special message form that featured in color and across the top an artist's representation of a hearty family of colonists bringing home a Christmas tree amid snow-covered New England hills.

> SAFE AND WELL / UNABLE TO PHONE /
> WILL KEEP YOU INFORMED /
> DON'T WORRY. MERRY XMAS TO ALL.
> ALICE ZWICKER

There was much Alice and her chums did not know that November. They did not know that General MacArthur had altered his theory as to when the Japanese would attack the Philippines, changing from spring to sometime after January. Admiral Hart, commander in chief of the U.S. Asiatic Fleet, had come to a more alarming and better-informed conclusion. He thought that the day of the Army-Navy Game, December 1, would be a likely time for a sneak attack.[12]

On November 24, General MacArthur received a message from Washington, DC, warning of a possible aggressive attack by the Empire of Japan. The following day, Admiral Stark, chief of naval operations, sent a message to his admirals in the Pacific. This communication was "to be considered a war warning."[13] MacArthur ordered a "full alert." Five days later, Japanese premier General Tojo directed his diplomats in Washington, DC, to keep negotiating, thus allowing time for the Japanese task force heading for Hawaii to arrive within striking distance.

Even if unaware of these facts, one could sense a growing tension. There were practice blackouts at Fort McKinley, and on Corregidor, gun crews were sleeping at their emplacements. Alice, who confessed she had a "pessimistic side," began to buy and lay aside necessities: soap, bath towels, nail polish, and lipstick—those things that might be very hard to procure if worse came to worst. Her Lieutenant Fred was now on board the USS *Maryanne*, patrolling the harbor and naval installations. He was sure that trouble was not far off.

Some seven months later, Alice copied these lines from the lyrics in a Tommy Dorsey song, "Sailing at Midnight":

> You're sailing at midnight
> I'll be on the shore . . .
> I long for your kiss
> I miss your caress . . .
> You're sailing at midnight.

Then, on the bright morning of December 8,[14] the peacetime world in the Pacific was shattered with word that Pearl Harbor, America's bastion in the Pacific and the port from which the fleet would supposedly sail to protect and relieve the Philippines, was under attack. Mildred Dalton was being measured for riding boots when she heard the news. Other nurses got a telephone call while they were on duty or were awakened by a bungalow mate.

When Alice heard, she thought how fortunate it was to have made arrangements for sending part of her check home. She had told her mother that as long as the checks kept coming, then the family would know she was all right. It seems strange, with everything at stake, that this thought seemed comforting to her.

The nurses at McKinley were issued World War I helmets and gas masks, along with identification tags.[15] They stood holding these cumbersome artifacts from another war and looking into each other's faces. It was like being told by a doctor that one's symptoms were really serious. In the faces of their sister nurses was disbelief that soon faded into bewilderment and resentment. In retrospect, those silent exchanges also held a deeper meaning, a sense of something that had been incipient in their choice of profession and developed in their training as nurses: It was the solidarity of caring, which, in the end, would preserve them through all of the horror to come.

Alice's bungalow mate, Minnie Breese, along with nurse Hattie Brantley, showed another indispensable attribute: practicality. There was no use wasting a beautiful afternoon. Let the generals decide what to do. They shoved their acquired helmets and gas masks into their golf bags and headed for the links.

In Brownville, Maine, Eli Zwicker was sitting with his father at the kitchen table listening to the radio. The program was interrupted with the news flash that Pearl Harbor had been bombed. They looked at each other, knowing that it meant war in the Pacific, and both immediately thought, "Alice!"

6

A WORLD RED WITH BLOOD AND FIRE

The war came to Fort McKinley with the sound of bombers in the night sky. Alfred Weinstein and his fellow doctors, interrupted in their run for the hospital, lay flattened on the veranda of their quarters. The target was nearby Nichols Field, but the gut-jarring thud of bombs seemed like near misses. There were Filipino troops camped on the golf course in front of the doctors' quarters; in frustration, they opened up with machine guns, rifles, and even .45s on the Japanese planes flying high and safely above. The night was filled with a pyrotechnic display of tracer bullets. It was incredible, but then the spent bullets fell back on the fort. Dr. Weinstein remembered them hitting the roof of his quarters with "ugly ripping sounds."[1]

The bombers made one pass and then were gone. The doctors continued their run toward the hospital. The nurses came like white wraiths hurrying through the darkness. The cry of ambulance sirens grew louder. They were bringing the wounded from Nichols Field.

Alice and her nursing comrades were unprepared for what that night would bring. Even if each nurse had previously served through some natural disaster, they would not have been ready for the continuing anguish and the growing fear and horror. Across Luzon, each medical team would have to come to grips with triage, trauma, and the preserving of life amid the ghastly, ongoing results of war.

At Fort McKinley Station Hospital, the sorting of the wounded began. Blood-clotted litters filled the corridors. There was a surreal quiet that Weinstein could not explain. Perhaps the casualties had already been sedated by the medics at Nichols Field; perhaps it was the efficient work of the nurses who filled large syringes with morphine and moved from patient to patient. Using a solution of green soap and saline, these young women who had brought their bathing suits to the Philippines began to clean dirt and grease from around red, gaping wounds and charred burns.

Alice scrubbed for one of the six operating rooms and entered under the glaring lights. The heat of the day remained in the operating pavilion. The surgeons changed gloves and worked on man after man. The nurses dabbed away sweat from the doctors' foreheads, anticipated the next instrument that would be needed, counted sponges, reeled off lengths of atraumatic intestinal catgut, monitored vital signs, and struggled to maintain a sterile field. The attack had come shortly after midnight, and the operating tables were in constant use until after three o'clock that morning.

Afterward, there was much that the nurses wished they could wrench from their memories. But memory is a part of learning, and sometimes what those grouped around the operating tables learned had a stomach-turning fascination. Many of the wounded, both Filipino and American, were infected with roundworms. One roundworm, as large as an "American earthworm," Weinstein remembered, crawled out from an intestinal perforation during repairs on a belly wound. After that, an inspection for roundworms was part of standard procedure.

The morning came, and daylight quickly warmed the white stucco walls of the hospital building. The facility stood as it had before: two-storied, surrounded by verandas, and under a solid-looking, red-tiled roof, but everything else had changed. For the next two nights, Alice and her nursing comrades slept fully dressed, what little sleep they had. Each day there were more casualties, more wounds to dress, more operations, more horror to be endured, and more comfort to be given. There were consecutive days during those peak arrivals of casualties when there would be no break.

Yet the redeeming certainty that relief was on the way remained persistent and omnipresent. The defenders went to look, expecting to see the Pacific Fleet steaming into Manila Harbor or friendly planes flying over the eastern horizon. They would be looking for months to come.

Alice and her friends did not know that a convoy of seven transports and freighters loaded with arms, troops, aviators, and planes, escorted by the heavy cruiser *Pensacola,* had been diverted en route to the Philippines and ordered to head for Australia. There was too little left to take any risks.

The officer who spoke to the nurses at Sternberg Hospital on the morning the war began was being honest when he said that no one knew what would happen:

> I want each one of you to remember that you are an American. You are an officer in the United States Army. This is an unusual situation, and we do not know what will happen. You know your duty and your responsibility. There may come a time when there is no one to tell you what to do and no one to guide you, but you will know what your conscience says, and you will know the oath you have taken to protect your country.[2]

That moment was too charged for a nurse to wonder why her rank was still considered "relative," why she was addressed as "Miss" and not as "Lieutenant," and why she need not be saluted. None of these facts had officially changed, but here amid this brewing hell she, as nurse and woman, was taking her place beside the men and the heroes.

From the onset, the war in the Philippines had been a disaster for the United States and its Philippine allies. Most disastrous had been the bombing of Clark Air Base on that first day of war. Twelve Flying Fortresses (B-17s) had been caught lined up on the ground and destroyed. Five more were severely damaged. Those long-range bombers were to have been the deterring force against a Japanese amphibious assault. Thirty Curtiss Warhawks (P-40s) were destroyed as well. In that one day, the U.S. Army Air Force in the Philippines was reduced to seventeen bombers and forty fighters.[3]

On December 10, the Rising Sun of Japan filled the sky. Thirty-five fighters scrambled to meet a screen of fifty-two Zeros, and when the American interceptors had been disposed of, the Japanese bombers flew unopposed over their targets: Nichols Field, Camp Murphy, and, with devastation, the naval base at Cavite. Navy nurse Margaret Nash would later tell of surgeons at Cavite standing in blood, of two or more casualties in one bed, and of others sitting in chairs holding onto their legs and arms, trying to stop their own bleeding.

With Japan as owner of the sky over Luzon, what was left of the U.S. Asiatic Fleet in the China Sea had to be pulled south and out of range, so the sea belonged to the Rising Sun as well. The Allied Army was left to fight unprotected from attacks by air or sea. On December 10, the Japanese landed troops at Aparri, on the northern tip of Luzon. It was not the major landing that would come eleven days later in the Lingayen Gulf, but it was fateful all the same.

There were no raids on December 11, as a monsoon buffeted the Japanese air bases on Formosa. The next day, when those bases cleared, the bombers were back to obliterate what was left at Cavite and to set parts of Manila ablaze.

—*୰*—

On December 13, the medical commander, Colonel James Duckworth, called the McKinley staff together. It was expected that Sternberg Hospital would be inundated with ten thousand casualties. To meet this exigency, Sternberg was being expanded by the establishment of a number of auxiliary facilities located around Manila. The list of sites included the Philippine Women's University, the Normal School for Women, De La Salle University, the Jai Alai sporting arena, and St. Scholastica's College. Fort McKinley would be evacuated, and its staff would be redistributed to help set up and staff these new facilities. Alice packed underwear, uniforms, and one dress. The rest of her clothes were boxed for the warehouse. It was the last she saw of those possessions.

Both Alice and Dr. Weinstein were assigned to Sternberg's new Annex E, St. Scholastica's, a relatively young Catholic institution founded for the education of poor young women. This cloistered establishment was (and is) situated close to the bay in a southern suburb of Manila, known as Malinta. It lies across Leon Guinto Street and a short distance east of De La Salle University and Taft Avenue.[4] The building occupied by the medical team from McKinley was a two-storied limestone and concrete structure with a red-tiled floor and barred windows. From its colonnaded verandas, one looked out on a pleasant patio and an extensive flower garden, but there was no time to enjoy these new surroundings. Assisted by sisters from the school, the medical team worked day and night to set up a hospital. Halls and classrooms became wards filled with metal cots. An operating pavilion took shape, and there the surgical teams waited for casualties.

Around them, Manila had become a city unhinged by war. The criminal element was abroad during the blackouts. The traffic tangled in the streets: carabao wagons, buses, pushcarts, and official cars that disregarded the traffic laws, if there were any left. Throngs of people were coming into the city seeking safety, mixed with crowds fleeing Manila for the countryside. Perhaps most dangerous were the jittery guards and sentries who, fed by the upwelling rumors of saboteurs, challenged and fired simultaneously.

Everything was in flux. Dr. Weinstein was ordered to set up the receiving station at the Normal School for Women in Manila. He set off in his Chrysler coupe while Alice remained with the small medical contingent at St. Scholastica's. They were soon busy enough. The wards and hallways increasingly filled with the critically wounded, many too seriously hurt to be moved again. Much to the relief of the staff, navy nurses evacuated from Canacco Hospital in Cavite arrived to help.

It becomes difficult to follow the lives of individuals as December 1941 stumbled on in an unbelievable defeat. On the 17th, the main

Japanese invasion fleet of some seventy-six transports put to sea and steamed for Luzon. It carried Lieutenant General Masaharu Homma's army of over forty-three thousand men, along with tanks, field artillery, and flamethrowers.

The screen of U.S. submarines failed to deter Homma's invasion, and the few bombers remaining were ineffective. Northward of Manila, the progress of the Japanese who had already landed was steady. They were battle-hardened troops used to mangling the Chinese, and they routed those Filipino troops for whom there had been too little time to train and prepare. In the midst of all this, intelligence reported that the Japanese would soon land in Lamon Bay, south of Manila, thus placing the city in a pincer between a collapsing front to the north and a new determined Japanese advance from the south.

General MacArthur withdrew his headquarters to the island fortress of Corregidor on December 23. He declared Manila an "open city," hoping to spare it from further pulverization. His aim had been to stop the enemy on the beaches, but time for preparation had run out, his air force was destroyed, and the Japanese spearhead, which had come ashore at Lingayen Bay, was pushing his forces back at a rate of some ten miles per day. Under these conditions, he adopted a plan that had existed since 1921, called War Plan Orange 3.[5] In this plan, the defending troops would withdraw onto the peninsula of Bataan, with the island fortress of Corregidor to back them, and there, in that rugged—even wild—topography, they would delay the enemy and protect Manila Bay until relief could come.

Under optimal conditions, withdrawal onto the peninsula of Bataan would necessitate an intricate operation. With no air cover and with their options limited to a single exposed route, its accomplishment was an amazing achievement, carried out with good soldiering and heroics in the field.

As MacArthur's staff feverishly worked to execute War Plan Orange, the wounded from Stotsenberg Hospital (near Clark Air Field) were evacuated seventy miles south, to Sternberg Hospital in Manila. At

Stotsenberg, nurse Helen Cassiani (Alice's companion, known to her many friends as "Cassie") was given a pistol, a green sock pendulous with ammunition, and, under the direction of a young sergeant, a brief practice session using a clump of large banana blossoms as a target. That done, Cassie was told that she was to be in charge of a railroad car loaded with wounded being evacuated to Manila.

Upon entering the city, the train came under an air raid, and the wounded, already traumatized by bombing and strafing, began to panic. Even amputees tried to leave the coach. Without her pistol, Cassie took a resolute stand in the doorway of the car and proclaimed in the strongest voice she could muster that no one was going anywhere.

It was a day stretched to the snapping point and filled with a dislocation of emotions. Word came that the Japanese, as expected, had landed seven thousand troops at Lamon Bay, south of Manila. When Cassie reached Sternberg Hospital on the 24th, she found herself in the midst of the shift in medical operations from Manila to Bataan. All previous preparations had become obsolete.

Just that day, twenty-four army nurses and one navy nurse, with an equal number of Filipina nurses, all dressed in white starched duty uniforms, had left for Bataan, clinging to seats in the back of trucks. One of these nurses, Hattie Brantley, described their garb: "white hose and shoes with World War I gas masks strapped to our waists and one of those shallow, World War I helmets balanced precariously atop each head." According to Hattie, there was one word that described them all: *unprepared*. Overhead, the enemy seemed to be everywhere. The nurses had to hit the roadside ditches several times on their route to Bataan.

To the nurses, their present patients in Manila came first, many of who were in need of critical care. But their duty also lay with those thousands of new casualties who would soon be crying for help in Bataan. There was a chance that many of the seriously wounded could be evacuated to Australia on the *Mactan*, an inter-island steamer adapted into a hospital ship of sorts. If that were to happen, both patients and boat needed to be prepared. In addition to patient care and preparation for evacuation, there was a crucial need to collect vital medical supplies and ship them to Bataan.

Across the battlegrounds in Luzon, crucial supplies of all kinds were being left behind in the Allied retreat. Paul Ashton, medical officer for the 21st Infantry Division, and later, chief surgeon at Hospital No. 1 in Bataan, went back to abandoned Fort McKinley. He was astonished to find warehouses stuffed with food and supplies. Among the medical supplies, Ashton and his men found boxes of surgical instruments and a thousand gold wafers intended for dental work. The gold wasn't of much use, but instruments and trucks left in the motor pool were. They loaded the trucks with essential supplies and commenced the arduous and dangerous trip back to Bataan.[6]

In the midst of what was precariously close to mayhem, Alice was sent back to Sternberg—to colonial Sternberg now with slit trenches dug amid the hibiscus flowers for the protection of staff and patients.[7] There, to some degree, the nursing team that had been together at Fort McKinley was still intact. Though they had worked together only briefly, they had strength in comradeship. They had gotten to know something of the abilities that lived inside each individual, and they knew each other by their nicknames. To the team, Alice was "Swish"; like all good nicknames, it fit her well, matching the way Alice danced, fitting the way she played sports, and describing the way she got things done.

Within this team natural leaders were emerging, like Frances Nash, whom Dr. Weinstein described as a "strapping, brown-haired, comely girl" who could whip an operating-room staff into shape.[8] She had received extensive experience in emergency rooms at Grady Hospital in Atlanta, Georgia, and her expertise was needed. On Christmas Eve, Colonel Duckworth told Frances that she was to stay on in Manila until medical staff members had been evacuated and supplies had been sent to either Corregidor or Bataan. "Prepare yourself," Duckworth warned Nash. "You may be taken prisoner." Frances, Alice, and all the nurses in Manila shared that danger as "Black Christmas" dawned.

Orders changed. On Christmas night, Nash, along with other nurses, was told to board a small steamer and head across Manila Bay to a second hospital being established on the peninsula of Bataan. As they left, the black water of the bay reflected the ruddy light of the burning city. Before Frances could find her place at Hospital No. 2, she was ordered by Duckworth to report to Dr. Weinstein at Hospital No. 1. She was to help set up an operating pavilion.

Alice worked on at Sternberg, collecting and packing medicine and equipment to be taken to Bataan. Around her, the number of army nurses steadily decreased as groups were evacuated to Corregidor or Bataan. On December 26, Cassie and six more nurses made the dangerous passage from Manila to Hospital No. 1. A person might be bombed or strafed crossing the bay, but there was no doubt of the impending and certain peril of capture if one stayed at Sternberg. The Japanese were closing in on General MacArthur's "open city."[9]

The few army nurses remaining in Manila were issued noncombatant identification cards to be used if they had to surrender. "Surrender? Surrender!" wrote Nurse Madeline Ullom, who received one of those cards. "The only surrender which entered my mind until now was [the name of] the favorite perfume of one of the nurses."

Alice would have gotten a kick out of Ullom's reaction.

Also given out were Red Cross armbands and men's overalls, size 42. The learning curve for the Army Nurse Corps in the Philippines had to be steep. When Alice arrived in Manila, the prevailing wisdom was that army nursing differed little from hospital service stateside. Now it was evident that white uniforms were obsolete in a war where nurses worked in near-front-line conditions.

Alice held up the pair of overalls handed to her; they looked like a shelter-half. Unlike her sisters, Alice had assiduously evaded learning how to sew. "I don't know how to sew a stitch," she used to say, "but I know how clothes ought to fit." Now she needed a tailor.

On the same day that Cassie left Manila, Alice received her orders to transfer to Hospital No. 1, twenty-five miles across Manila Bay. She arrived at Limay on the east coast of Bataan in a barge loaded with collected medical supplies. It was one o'clock on the morning of December 27.[10] The large mass of a tin-sheathed warehouse stood above the beach, dully metallic in the moonlight, like some ominous stronghold in a Gothic novel. (See the Map of Bataan in the photospread.)

Limay was a village of huts built on stilts and situated two-thirds of the way down Bataan's east coast and on the only road running forty-two miles down the Bataan peninsula to its tip, and the port of Mariveles. When the medical teams came to set up their hospitals, four-fifths of the peninsula was jungle forest punched upward thousands of feet by two extensive and, at the time, inactive volcanoes: Mount Natib (3,052 feet), filling the peninsula's north except for the coastal area on Manila Bay; and Mount Mariveles (4,700 feet), filling the southern end.

The road that ran past Limay to Mariveles continued its tortuous route roughly two-thirds of the way up the west coast of the peninsula, to end at the village of Moran. There was one cobblestone road, which ran between the two mountains and across the peninsula from Bagac on the west to Pilar on the east, a distance of perhaps twenty-four miles. This was the peninsula of Bataan, which the creators of War Plan Orange had selected as the place for a last holdout should Japan victoriously attack the Philippines.

Perhaps Alice already knew that this was a place notorious for its malignant contagion of malaria and dengue fever.

7

BATAAN

It was a short night for Alice. As she stood on the porch of the nurses' quarters, the morning light disclosed the full extent of Hospital No. 1.

She had been warned to expect rustic facilities. Many of the nurses who had arrived three days earlier had been taken by surprise. Leona Gastinger had exclaimed, "This is a hospital?" She spoke for all the nurses climbing down from the backs of the trucks that had brought them from Manila. They had expected to find a medical facility similar to those in which they had been trained. Some had been told it would have a thousand beds, but here, under nipa-thatched and corrugated iron roofs, were little more than sheds![1]

The nurses' quarters and officers' mess shared a single-story wooden building situated on the south end of the fenced-off grounds. From the screened porch of the nurses' quarters, one looked over a large quadrangle to the surgery pavilion and, behind that, to a row of warehouses that obscured the view to Manila Bay. On each side of the quadrangle was a row of rough buildings, eight on a side, which had served as barracks when the facility had been a training camp for Philippine Scouts. These structures were now being scrubbed down and converted into wards. Some already had patients—sick soldiers from Manila who were to be sent to the front lines as soon as they were well enough.

In front of the mess hall a large Red Cross insignia made from bed-sheets was pinned to the ground. Behind the barracks and around the periphery of the camp was a line of support buildings: laundry, latrines, noncommissioned mess halls, and a water tower that was filled from an artesian well.

Despite the miracles wrought by the engineers in installing a genera-tor, stringing electric lines, and installing flush toilets, this was still a jungle hospital. When Alice met up with surgeon Dr. Alfred Weinstein, he was not encouraging. He thought it was a "lousy setup." To Alice the only certain fact was that here among the mango and tall bamboo trees, she was ten thousand miles from home, and the world was becoming a hell of a mess.

But there was no time to pause; Alice had orders to report to the surgical building.

Hattie Brantley, whom Alice had known at Fort McKinley, and who was in the first contingent of nurses to reach Limay, described what they found upon arrival.

They had accomplished much since that night before Christmas. Equipment for a thousand-bed general hospital had been stored in one of the Limay warehouses. To begin with, before they could start to un-pack the medical equipment, the nurses had to locate the disassembled parts for their own cots and then lug these parts nearly the length of the camp to the nurses' quarters. Hattie swore that the cot parts were wrapped in newspapers from 1918. Once the cots were set up, they had to traipse back to the warehouse for their mattresses and bedding.

The next day (Christmas Day), they began to hunt through unmarked cartons for hospital equipment, from bedpans to thermometers. The surgical instruments had been coated with the preservative Cosmoline, which resisted all solvents at hand with the exception of ether. There were some woozy nurses before the needed instruments were cleaned. "We may need that ether we used before we're done," Hattie observed.

The operating pavilion had once been a barroom. The scrubbing and cleaning was still going on when Alice arrived. The space (fourteen by forty feet) was large enough for eight operating tables. Searchlights were being mounted on poles to provide illumination. The instruments were to be placed on a central table and covered with a sterile sheet. From this store, the surgical nurses from each team would select what they needed.

They all knew that the deluge of wounded could begin at any time. They worked hard on one of the hottest days Alice had experienced since her arrival in the Philippines. In the evening, Alice and her nurse friends took a break and walked the short distance to a small store in the village of Limay, where they had Coca-Cola for sale. For Alice and many other nurses who had grown up in small towns, it seemed a bit like home.

The wounded began arriving in growing numbers after New Year's Day. The Japanese attacked with fanatical ferocity, and the Allies withdrew painfully toward Bataan, becoming concentrated on the few available routes onto the peninsula. The Japanese air force took full advantage of this situation. The key Layla Bridge on the road onto the peninsula was blown by the retreating engineers, and some eighty thousand American and Filipino soldiers and twenty-six thousand fleeing civilians were left crowded onto the peninsula. Dr. John Bumgarner, who served on Bataan, wrote in his *Parade of the Dead*: "Never before had American forces been forced into such a pocket of misery." Inevitably, what was to follow was defeat by a relentless enemy, who controlled the air and sea, greatly assisted by hunger and disease.[2] No worse disaster had ever befallen American troops. The heroics of the defenders of Bataan had little to do with who lost or won.

By February 8, 1942, the defenders would be "dug in" in a line across the peninsula, from Mauban on the west coast to Mobatang on Manila Bay. Mount Natib, over three thousand feet high, rose in the center of that line (see the Map of Bataan in the photospread). The Japanese artillery and planes blasted in preparation for wave upon wave of infantry. Fourteen miles south, Hospital No. 1 at Limay was soon to be pressed hard with critical casualties.[3]

World War I had taught the Medical Corps a brutal lesson: Most of the wounded who died did so from bleeding and shock. Rapid treatment made a tremendous difference. The medics along the front line were to slow blood loss, pour sulfonamide powder into wounds, and administer morphine. Operational plans called for battalion aid stations some five hundred yards behind the front lines. They were to control hemorrhaging, treat shock, close chest wounds, and apply splints. Collecting stations, perhaps a mile to the rear, were to send those who needed emergency surgery and critical attention to field hospitals, five miles or so from the fighting. General hospitals, where extensive treatment would be performed, were to be located largely out of harm's way. This was the expected procedure.[4]

But this was Bataan, with its jungle trails and corkscrew road where ambulances, when they existed, were often forced to travel at night for fear of being strafed. There was no medical backup for the two newly established hospitals on Bataan, unless one considered Fort Mills Station Hospital on Corregidor, and that facility had enough problems as it was.[5] Hospital No. 1 was left to handle the surgical needs of the wounded who arrived there.

A new chapter in the saga of the Army Nurse Corps was about to be written, and a new estimation of the ability and courage of women nurses was materializing. Two nurses at Hospital No. 1 were to be seriously wounded. It was a miracle that all those nurses who struggled on Bataan came back home. Lest we forget, during World War II, 207 nurses did not.

Throughout January, as the Japanese blasted southward, increasing numbers of wounded arrived from the bloody cane fields on the eastern portion of the line, and from the jungle-fought battles of the "points" and "pockets" on the west.[6] (See the Map of Bataan in the photospread.)

Alice's friend, navy nurse Ann Bernatitus, wrote that sometimes those around the operating tables worked hard and "then again took life easy," but she was writing to an anxious Zwicker family back in Maine. There were respites, but more often the nurses worked harder than they had thought possible, and sometimes for days at a time. Nurses working around the operating tables reported that they had to step over the wounded who were waiting for attention. On January 16, when the Japanese breached the Allied line, there were 187 major surgical procedures in one day.[7]

In an oft-quoted passage from *Barbed-Wire Surgeon*, Dr. Weinstein graphically describes the sounds within the operating pavilion at Hospital No. 1:

> Sounds familiar to the operating pavilion vibrated through the air: the zzz-zzz-zzz of a saw as it cuts through bone, the rasp of a file as the freshly cut end, dripping red marrow, was ground smooth, the plop of an amputated leg dropping into a bucket, the grind of a rounded burr drill eating through a skull, the tap, tap of a small mallet on a chisel gouging out a shell fragment deeply imbedded in bone, the hiss of the sterilizer blowing off steam, the soft patter of nurses feet scurrying back and forth, the snip of scissors cutting through muscle, the swish of the mop on the floor cleaning up blood, strangling, gasping, irregular respiration of soldiers with chest wounds; the shallow, soft, faint breathing of those under smooth anesthesia; the snap of rubber gloves on outstretched hands, the rustle of operating gowns being changed, the shuffle of feet as weary surgeons and nurses shift their weight from one leg to another.[8]

No bombs landed on the hospital at Limay, but Japanese planes were often overhead and hitting targets nearby. At first, when planes came in low, operating teams had ducked, holding their gloved hands above their heads in an attempt to avoid contamination; later, they went on operating without a pause. As one surgeon said, "If they kill me, they kill me at work."

Like the dry-season dust that blew through the hospital compound and accumulated on everything, there was stress and anguish in every corner of the nurses' lives. Nurse Juanita Redmond, looking back at those days and nights, wrote: "Faced by so much suffering and death, something cracks inside you; you can't ever be quite the same."[9] Perhaps

she was thinking of that black night when she stooped over a soldier lying on a stretcher amid those awaiting help. He was dead. She turned
her flashlight on others nearby and found them dead as well.

Memories haunted Alice years later, as they did the other nurses
who had served with her. When some wounded Japanese were brought
to the surgical unit, they had multiple American wristwatches on their
arms. There were names engraved on those watches that the nurses
knew from their dancing days in Manila.

Then there were the questions that did not go away. Could that leg,
that eye, that life, have been saved, if there had been time and the
necessary expertise? Often in Alice's mind there appeared those dirty,
sweat-streaked, bloody faces that looked upward asking without words,
"Am I going to make it?"

"You can't go through what we went through and not be changed," Alice later told an audience. And there were draining worries: Would the
morphine supply last, what would happen when the quinine was gone,
and what would happen if the Japanese overran the hospital? Would the
nurses be raped and killed like the poor nuns in Nanking?

What the medical people on Bataan achieved amid the mayhem and
the unceasing demand was magnificent. Apparently it was a war correspondent struggling to express what he had witnessed who fortuitously
hit upon the phrase "Angels of Bataan" to describe the fifty-four nurses
on the peninsula. What they and their medical colleagues achieved is
reflected in the following statistic: Although Hospital No. 1 treated
1,200 casualties in twenty-nine days, there were only sixty-four crosses
left in the hospital's cemetery when the hospital was pulled back from
the immediate front.

By February 1942, the Allies were fighting an insidious combination
of three enemies: the Japanese and the grim twins of hunger and disease. In mid-February, Alice had a high fever and headache, and her
joints became inflamed. It was dengue fever, a mosquito-transmitted
disease that, like malaria, was becoming widespread on Bataan. She was
somewhat better in a week, but the lasting fatigue was frightening. She
found that by bracing herself on the operating table she could keep go-

ing. Later that year she was troubled with bronchitis and sinusitis. Still later, her legs would swell as she developed beriberi. She would later contract bacterial dysentery,[10] but escaped the great scourge of the Philippine struggle, malaria.

Although malaria was always a persistent problem in Bataan, it became epidemic in January 1942, when fighting moved into the low valleys south of Abucay. It is estimated that 37 percent of the frontline troops had been infected by March. During the first week of that month, there were five hundred hospital admissions of malaria-ridden patients. By the end of that month, the number of infected soldiers was between 75 and 80 percent. This increase paralleled the depletion of quinine necessary for both a prophylactic measure and a treatment. The quinine tablets bravely brought in by a P-40 fighter from Cebu helped those critically ill in the hospitals, but the lack of quinine was devastating for the troops. The half-starved medical staff was not immune. At Hospital No. 2, 60 percent of the staff suffered from malaria.[11]

On January 5, at the start of the defense of Bataan, rations were cut by half; by the middle of February, medical teams were seeing symptoms of malnutrition—apathy, irritability, diarrhea, and dysentery. Daily rations that month amounted to two thousand calories; by February, the daily allotment was 1,500, and by March, one thousand calories per day. This latter figure was three thousand calories short of what a soldier on the front line needed.

The debilitating consequences of near starvation, however, were not due to low caloric intake alone; the lack of crucial vitamins was also devastating. Even the rice, which was a staple in the available diet, had been milled and thus stripped of the essential vitamin B, or thiamine. In their patients and themselves, the medical personnel began to encounter the signs of this deficiency: vertigo, rapid pulse, severe intestinal pain, and swelling of the legs, all signs of beriberi. Chief Nurse Edith Shacklette told her nurses, "If necessary, we will have one meal every two days. I know you won't complain."[12]

As the casualties kept coming into Hospital No. 1, Alice struggled to maintain her concentration in the heat, and through one operation after another. Everyone gave more than she thought she had to give. On the wards there were forty, then sixty patients to one nurse. Maintaining sanitation became extremely difficult.[13] Every task was hard.

Hattie Brantley, changing dressings, went from patient to patient on her knees because it was too painful to straighten up. At times, members of the hospital and surgical staff slept at their posts to be immediately available. A few miles away, Hospital No. 2, overwhelmed with medical cases, hacked out new wards under the jungle canopy. As the crowding grew, the hospital's admissions were limited to only the critically wounded and sick. Nearer the front, collecting and clearing stations became field hospitals. In the end, there may have been some twelve thousand Allied casualties on Bataan, but before those last desperate days, there came a lull in the fighting that lasted from mid-February to the last week in March.

The Japanese had anticipated being in control of Luzon and Manila Bay by the end of January; here it was February, and they were stalemated halfway down the peninsula of Bataan. Disease had been a problem for them as well, and casualties had been unexpectedly heavy.[14] For General Homma, the failure to sweep the Allies from Bataan was a loss of face. The need to pause for reinforcements did not affirm Japan's position as leader of the Greater East Asia Co-Prosperity Sphere. Time was on Homma's side, however. Japanese reinforcements poured in— some twenty-two thousand men and an assortment of arms, including 240mm howitzers and huge siege mortars.[15] In the meantime, the Allies grew thinner and sicker.

Colonel James Duckworth, chief at Hospital No. 1, was a six-foot-plus, no-nonsense commander who did what he intended to do, which included his decision to move Hospital No. 1 further to the rear and out of immediate danger.[16] He might have waited had he known that there was a lull in the offing, but he did not know, and he was right that the hospital had to be moved. In a major feat, Hospital No. 1 was relocated under battle conditions in just two days and one night, without losing a single patient. Juanita Redmond remembered the great concern the staff evinced for the critically wounded and how those soldiers would ask if their wounded buddy had survived the move. To Alice, it seemed an exhausting blur: operating, packing, moving, unpacking, and operating again.

They called the new location "Little Baguio," because its climate was reminiscent of Baguio, the summer capital of Luzon, and a resort where people went to get away from the heat. The new hospital site was situated high above the southern coast on the slopes that rose to Mount Bataan (see the Map of Bataan in the photospread). The cooling winds from the sea blew through tall hardwoods, and the place was nearly mosquito-free. Like the site at Limay, the two acres chosen at Little Baguio had existing buildings.[17] In the case of Little Baguio, these buildings had served as garages, repair shops, and barracks for an army motor pool.

At the center of the assemblage was a large, wood-framed building that became the surgery and Ward 9 for malaria patients. North and across the road from this building were six shed-like garages, closely grouped. These became wards. West of the wards and higher up were two buildings that housed the officers' mess, nurses' quarters, and Ward 7. The hospital plan shows the commanding officer's quarters next to the annex for Ward 7; however, Colonel Duckworth appears to have had his own small travel trailer farther up the rise, and under what is described as a tall pine.[18] The officers' quarters were situated above and to the southwest of the nurses' quarters.

At first, Alice did not have an opportunity to appreciate the advantages of this new situation, except for the fact that it was mercifully cooler. The surgical work went on unabated at Little Baguio until the fighting slackened in mid-March and some degree of normalcy returned. There was time for the nurses to save cardboard and make playing cards for their patients. Dr. Weinstein wrote that romance began to flower with "an intensity and overpowering quality never experienced in leisurely peacetime life. . . . While death was closing in on all sides, we clung frantically to life."[19]

There was no end of rumors, including those that persisted in their claim that help was just over the horizon. Sometimes there were individuals who had a better idea of what was really happening.

Lieutenant Claude Fraleigh of the Dental Corps was such a fellow. Claude was gifted. He had been transferred from the USS *Canopus* and had organized the building of additional facilities at Hospital No. 1.[20] It is not clear whether Alice had met Fraleigh in Manila, but they were friends at Little Baguio. Through his connections with the *Canopus*, Alice may have learned news of Fred Newell and the *Maryanne*. Her Fred had seen some desperate action that was to lead to his being awarded the Navy Cross. He was still alive, the *Maryanne* still afloat.

The story of the USS *Canopus* is one of the bright spots in the darkly tragic defeat on Bataan. It was a 373-foot submarine tender assigned to the Asiatic Fleet and Manila Bay. With the destruction of Cavite Navy Yard near Manila, the tender was sent to Mariveles Bay on Bataan's southern coast, where it was hit by bombs on two occasions. To prevent its complete destruction, the ship was disguised as an abandoned hulk, complete with burning smudge pots to provide smoke. Belowdecks, the *Canopus* was very much alive, serving as a creative machine shop and arms builder for the defense of Bataan. In small groups, nurses were invited to come to the *Canopus* to take a shower and then enjoy an evening meal, served with silver on a white tablecloth. It was one of those rare moments when heaven touched the scorched earth.

Chief Nurse Josephine Nesbit had told the "girls" under her that she expected them to look like women, even under Bataan conditions. Even before this order, Alice intended to do so, as did most of the other nurses when they had a chance. In those few weeks of relative quiet, dances were planned. Cosmetics and perfume came out of hiding.

Alice's roommate at Little Baguio, Ann Bernatitus, had brought along a pair of high-heeled pumps, but she nearly fell when she tried to walk in them. Alice consoled her. She might have killed herself had she worn them on the improvised dance floor, where old blankets had been stretched and fastened over the bamboo floors. Alice and Ann decided that the best thing to wear on their feet were old socks.

For music, Claude Fraleigh, with his usual finesse, had found a pile of records from the 1920s. Alice was disappointed when she found that she and everyone else were too tired to jitterbug, but dancing is dancing, and it was something to be thankful for. When a dance was held in the officers' mess, a medic banged out the music on a broken-down piano. For added entertainment, Filipina nurses performed a native dance.

People remembered Alice's joking, her singing at the piano, her delight in dancing, and the way she covered trouble with a smile, but for Alice anguish was no less real. She kept praying that Lieutenant Newell, strong and handsome, would materialize from the night. He didn't.[21] Months later, when Alice was copying the lyrics for "There's a Lull in My Life," she wrote the annotation: "And how!"

> Oh, there's a lull in my life
> It's just a void and empty space
> When you are not in my tomorrow
> Oh, there's a lull in my life.

During the break in the fighting, there were parties held at Little Baguio as well, like the twenty-fifth birthday party that Helen Cassiani (Cassie) gave for herself and her friends, utilizing a hoarded bottle of Johnnie Walker Red, and the swimming party that Dr. Weinstein describes vividly:

> We piled into cars and hospital trucks for a trip over the new dirt road. On a bluff overlooking the dazzling white sandy strip, we could see Corregidor doggedly hunched in the sea while a flight of Nip planes made a run over it. . . . A footpath zigzagged down to the beach. It was a mass of barbed-wire entanglement and razor-edge bamboo poles sunk into the sand and their ends pointing seaward. . . . Changing our clothes in the underbrush, we gingerly made our way through the barricades, guided by smiling members of the Filipino Army detachment. We whooped and galloped happily down the gently sloping beach and dove into the calm, blue tropical waters.[22]

While four PT boats kept guard a few hundred yards off the beach, the medical personnel ate carabao sandwiches that the nurses had made, swam, and played like teenagers. Several of the men were very zealous in trying to teach a few nurses how to swim.

Much got crowded into those few weeks before once again the gates of hell burst open. Nurses from Hospital No. 2 made a visit to see the women at Little Baguio. There were visits to Corregidor as well, and then General Homma hurled his rebuilt forces at the Allies. He took no chances of further delay, and may not have realized how close the Allies were to physical collapse. Making use of the effects of the dry season, the Japanese began dropping phosphorous bombs and setting fire to the countryside along the Allies' defensive lines. The resulting burns were horrible. The operating tables were once again in constant use.

The hunger among the defenders grew. When Weinstein asked what the unidentifiable stew meat was, he was told, "Twenty-Seventh Cavalry." They were eating the horses, lucky to have any meat at all. Everything was running low. Used dressings were being washed and used again.

However pleasant the location of the hospital at Little Baguio, it was unfortunate in one major aspect: The site was wedged between targets too tempting for the Japanese and their newly acquired twin-engine bombers to ignore. Just to the south of the hospital area was the storage and staging base for the all-important army engineers, and to the north was the major ordnance storage for the Second Corps. Even if the Japanese had intended to honor the Red Cross emblems painted on the roofs of the hospital buildings and laid out on the ground, precision bombing was an ability of the future. It was only a matter of time before the hospital would be hit.

Along with another nurse and a doctor, Alice had jumped into a foxhole during one of the increasingly frequent and close bombings: "We were all trying to make light of it—we had to because we were so scared," Alice wrote. She kept rubbing her hands together until the doctor said, "Alice, why don't you take a cigarette? If you don't, you won't have any palms left on your hands." Alice smoked the offered cigarette and found it gave her something to do with her hands, so she joined the ranks of smokers.[23]

As the bombings increased, the foxholes became all too familiar to the nurses on Bataan. The bombers had been active all morning, hitting

targets very close by, and Alice and Juanita Redmond had been in and
out of foxholes between dashes to attend to their medical duties. As the
planes returned again, Alice yelled, "Red, for heaven's sake, get back in
that hole and put your helmet on."

In her book, Redmond remembered that it was "crowded, damp, and
dark in the foxhole," and that "Zwick kept saying over and over, 'Oh,
God, send them away.'" The moment the drone of the planes receded,
Alice jumped from the hole, shaking her fist at the disappearing planes.
"You'd better not come back," she yelled, and then there followed a
flood of expletives that would have made proud the best cusser among
the railroaders in Brownville. According to Redmond, Alice turned on
her foxhole buddies when they began to laugh. "I don't see a damn thing
that's funny!" she exclaimed.[24]

Alice was right. There wasn't anything funny about it.

Along the battle line the situation grew in brutality. The final assault
by the troops of the Rising Sun began on April 3, Good Friday, with a
heavy five-hour artillery shelling of the Allied positions. It is said that
windows rattled in Manila thirty miles away.

By coincidence, this was also the date that Alice managed to get a
telegraph message off to her parents. The island of Cebu was still in
American hands and had a telegraph station that could reach Pearl
Harbor. A precarious connection had been maintained between the
American forces on the Philippines and Cebu by means of two P-40s
and a ragtag assortment of salvaged planes.[25] Perhaps Claude Fraleigh
or Fred Newell, whose USS *Maryanne* was based at Port Mariveles,
assisted Alice; however it was accomplished, the telegram got transmit-
ted. It read: "Safe and well. Keep you informed. If possible, reply RCA.
Alice Zwicker."

Mary, James, and all the Zwickers still in Maine treasured that message, but Alice was not safe or well, and she knew it.

In a thundering moment on the morning of March 30, the glass in the
nurses' quarters was blown in as a bomb hit just outside. Stunned by the
blast, Alice fought to regain her equilibrium amid the shards of glass,
shrapnel-ripped walls, and swirling dust.

Dr. Weinstein was sound asleep after working most of the night when a bomb demolished one of the wings of the officers' quarters. He ran for a drainage ditch.

The greatest explosion came when a bomb made a direct hit on a truck loaded with artillery ammunition as it was passing the entrance to the hospital. Colonel Duckworth had been knocked down. He might well have been killed; it was a near thing. He was up, holding a fire extinguisher under his arm, and trying to put out a fire when Weinstein made his dash for the operating rooms.

Twenty-three patients and Filipino orderlies were killed in the attack. The Japanese apologized, but many at Little Baguio thought the bombing was deliberate. Whatever the truth, this attack was just a prelude to the bloody havoc that was to come.

The wounded kept arriving. In Weinstein's words, the casualties were "haggard, hungry, dehydrated, and bled-out." There may have been nearly 4,500 patients in Hospital No. 1 at this time. Space had run out, and the casualties were lying under the trees. On the morning of April 7, Nurse Hattie Brantley had been sent to lay out a new ward of rough-fashioned triple bunks under a huge acacia tree. She was there at about 10:00 a.m. when Japanese bombs fell again.

A large bomb[26] dropped through the lightly fabricated roof of the annex to Ward 5, the ward where Hattie would have been. The devastation was terrible. Hattie returned to the screams of the wounded, and re-wounded. Nurses and orderlies worked frantically to extricate those still alive from the wreckage. Later, one of the corpsmen climbed a nearby tree to bring down a dangling body.[27] Two nurses were wounded: Rosemary Hogan, her face covered with blood, and Rita Palmer, with shrapnel in her chest and legs, her clothes all but blown away. In remembering that horrible day, Juanita Redmond speaks of trying to shut her ears to the "scraping of spades" digging graves.

Among the patients were seventy-three killed and 117 re-wounded, sixteen of whom later died. The casualties would have been greater except for the work of orderlies and nurses in the orthopedic ward, who, during the bombing, cut the traction lines, freeing patients to get under their beds or into a foxhole if they were able. Operating went on all that day, with Dr. Weinstein swearing in Yiddish and Alice wet with sweat.

The day before the bombing, April 6—the day after Easter—the Allies had made one last counterattack. There was no way it could be sustained, and the Japanese advanced to within a few miles of Hospitals No. 1 and 2. As someone remarked, those two facilities now resembled the scene in *Gone with the Wind* when the wounded were laid out in Atlanta's railroad yard.

Then, quite suddenly it seemed, at around dusk on April 8, Colonel Duckworth ordered the nurses to gather only essentials and assemble for immediate evacuation. Like those fleeing from a house on fire, the nurses took an assortment of things, not all of which were necessities. One nurse left her underwear on the line.

What was to trouble every nurse for the rest of their lives was the leaving behind of their patients. It troubled them deep down, where the reality of their nurse's oath had come to live. Years later, Nurse Frankie Lewey met one of the men she had nursed on Bataan. "Fine angel I was," she exclaimed, "leaving you there on Bataan in a body cast."

All of those young men had been so wonderful. Hattie Brantley remembered a young man who had lost all his limbs in a mine explosion. She used to visit him as often as she could. He had said to her, "You shouldn't be undergoing such hardships." Minnie Breese remembered the eyes of her patients, saying, "Those eyes just followed us."[28]

The nurses had been ordered to leave Bataan. The doctors and members of the medical staff gathered around as they climbed onto the battered buses. They wished them Godspeed and shared again that mantra of consolation—the assurance that help would come.

The lurid night seemed to have engaged Dante to write its text. As the buses inched along the crooked, narrow road to the port of Mariveles, the Allies on Bataan were surrendering. The night sky burst and glowed with fire as everything that might be of use to the Japanese was being destroyed; beaten soldiers and frantic civilians clogged the road toward the sea. Some civilians beat on the bus and begged to be taken aboard. This entire frantic and dispirited nightmare was cloaked in

rising dust, which Hattie Brantley remembered gave a "ghostly appearance to the entire landscape."[29]

Colonel Carlos Romulo turned his head as the vehicles carrying the
nurses crept by: "I could not bear to look into their faces. . . . I knew
what was written on them. . . . It was something more dreadful than fear
because it was active. It was inevitability. . . . I will never forgive the
fact that American women under the American flag had to know that
night—the last night in Bataan."

Alice wrote her own brief account of that night:

> The evacuation of Bataan was like something I'd seen in a movie.
> Newsreels of the countries in Europe and people evacuating before the
> onslaught of Hitler's armies. This could be the same thing. Philippine
> refugees hurrying, they knew not where, with their few meager belong-
> ings and their carabao carts. It's heavy jungle all around and the roads
> practically impassable.
>
> What a night! The Japs bombing the area. Corregidor was shelling Cab-
> caben where the Japs had made a landing, and the Japs were returning
> the fire. The Army was blowing up ammunition dumps and the Navy was
> scuttling any ships it had and blowing up the Navy tunnels that they had
> been occupying while on Bataan. Nothing was to be left to the Japs. In the
> middle of all this there was an earthquake!
>
> I had hated to go to the Rock [Corregidor] actually, because I did not
> want to be cooped up in those tunnels. It was rough being outside and to
> take the beating we had taken, but I felt that it would be worse to be inside
> and underground. As we neared the Navy Depot at [Mariveles, which was
> a few kilometers away from Little Baguio, but over a steep mountain road],
> with the world bursting at the seams around us, I thought—what next!
>
> We got to the dock and were told that an inter-island boat would pick
> us up in about an hour to take us to Corregidor. Well, we sure were sitting
> ducks in that spot.[30] But I was so tired that I put my barracks bag under
> my head, adjusted my helmet, and made one last request: "Somebody be
> sure to wake me up when the boat comes, because I'm going to take five."
> I wasn't brave, just beat. And so amidst all the fury of war I went to sleep.

Nurse Helen "Cassie" Cassiani describes being packed with the other
nurses into a "small launch," some "sitting on their luggage, some on the

bottom of the boat, others on [the] boat's gunwales." They had grown used to the explosions in the night, and then there was a "deafening explosion . . . echoing and re-echoing against the cliffs surrounding the harbor"[31] as tunnels above the harbor were destroyed. Ahead, the venerable old *Canopus* was being scuttled. She was aflame, and her magazines were exploding.

Then, as if the rock of the earth itself was being convulsed, there was an earthquake. The launch rocked in the resulting waves and the reflection of flame rode up and down on the black sea.

As Alice remembered, they reached the dock at Corregidor about 3:00 a.m.

—◦◦◦—

Back at Little Baguio, what was left of the medical staff awaited the will of the Japanese. As Dr. Weinstein walked toward the surgery, his mind returned to the weeks that had passed:

> The operating pavilion, sturdy throbbing heart of the hospital, had ceased beating, its shrapnel-pocked walls and loosened joints and beams bearing mute testimony to the shellacking it had received. . . . The soft patter of Filipino nurses as they circulated about the loaded operating tables could still be heard. The wisecracks of New England's gum-chewing, happy-go-lucky Miss Zwicker still echoed on the listless air.[32]

8

CORREGIDOR

The island of Corregidor was under blackout. After the pyrotechnics the nurses had passed through, the darkness was impenetrable. The nurses from Bataan stood on the island's north dock and waited for some conveyance to their new station in Malinta Tunnel.

The shape of Corregidor Island is often described as a four-mile-long pollywog swimming out of Manila Bay. The port area on the island is situated at the place where the pollywog's "tail" is connected to the "body." To the east of the port is Malinta Hill, whose massive rock formation is penetrated by Malinta Tunnel, running through its center. To the west, rising to 550 feet above the ocean, are the heights occupied by Fort Mills (see the Map of Corregidor in the photospread).

Fort Mills had been designed and constructed in the dreadnought era, a fact that is reflected in the names given to the fort's two areas. The highest area was called "Topside." Located on Topside were the headquarters, the parade ground, and the two-story stone barracks, which may have been the longest barracks building in the world. The area lower down the hill was known as "Middleside." Fort Mills Station Hospital was located there, along with other facilities. Appropriately, the harbor area was designated "Bottomside." Topside and Middleside were ringed with eleven major gun batteries, not counting the antiair-craft installations and the two concrete pits holding the twelve-inch mortars. These latter installations were old, but they were to give the Japanese a fair amount of grief.[1]

As part of Corregidor's defenses, Malinta Tunnel was built as a shell- and bombproof shelter to house communications, a command post, supplies, and a hospital. Between the years 1922 and 1932,[2] an 830-foot main tunnel was blasted through the volcanic rock, along with twenty-four side laterals. The engineers were American, the foremen Philippine Scouts, and the workers, Filipino convicts. The TNT used to blast the passageways was an old powdered variety that had to be rolled into cartridges by hand. The tracks of an electric railroad that ran through the main tunnel connected the tunnel complex with the harbor. This railroad then wound its way up the hill to Fort Mills, ending at the westernmost batteries, which looked out on the China Sea.

Evidently, the tunnel planners realized that the hospital at Middle-side was exposed to shelling and bombing. As a result, a rectangular grid of twelve vaulted ceiling tunnels was cut deep within Malinta Hill. These hospital tunnels were connected to the main tunnel by one of the laterals, and had their own connection to the outside world through a portal known as the North Entrance. Each of the hospital tunnels was 160 feet long and fifteen feet wide.

For over ten weeks, this tunnel complex, which housed the wards, operating facilities, and pharmacy, became the enclosed, reverberat-ing, stifling, and sometimes utterly pitch-black "home" of the nurses from Bataan. Speaking of those times of darkness when the power was interrupted, Hattie Brantley commented, "If you ever wanted to feel what the darkness of the Egyptian pyramids must have been like, you should have been in Malinta Tunnel when the lights went out."[3] General Wainwright spoke of a "Stygian darkness" when the power failed. The tunnels were "home" as well for those nurses who had been stationed at Fort Mills Hospital on Middleside before the bombing had begun. The combined number of nurses was now eighty-five, not counting the twenty-six Filipino nurses.

Malinta Tunnel was an impressive feat of engineering, but it was not intended to house large numbers of people, and, as the weeks went on, its environment became "almost intolerable. Dust, dirt, great black flies, and vermin were everywhere, and through everything permeated the odor of the hospital and human bodies."⁴ Eric Morris in *Corregidor* describes the tunnel's atmosphere thus: "The smell of mildew, urine, and sweat mingled with the fumes of the diesel engines that powered the generators."⁵

For a time, many of those in the tunnels got outside to enjoy the sweet wafting breezes of tropical nights. Sometimes there was singing, songs like "The Yellow Rose of Texas" or "Home on the Range,"⁶ and a couple might drift away together, into the bushes. But there were fewer and fewer bushes to be found as the withering, searing bombardment went on. As Alice was to note, it became safer to stay within the protection of the Rock, and to put up with the deteriorating conditions inside the tunnel maze.

Not least amid the extraordinary service and heroism that characterized the defense of Corregidor was the work of engineers and the quartermaster's department. They kept the electrical power system going, drilled for water, and jury-rigged new hospital wards (by the first week in May there were 1,500 patients). When General MacArthur moved his headquarters to the Rock, it was these engineers who established toilet facilities within the tunnel. However, there were problems they could not fix. One of these was the inadequate ventilation system, an issue that was to become truly serious as the hive-like population grew. Even before the influx of human beings, during the dry season, walls had dripped with moisture. Despite this condensing moisture, a sifting of gritty concrete dust fell and floated after each concussion.

Those within the tunnels reported losing a sense of reality. Alice wrote:

It's hard to realize that life was ever the peaceful, pleasant living of the tropics. It has been a long time since war began in the Philippines, or so it seems. . . . Is it possible that I came from a small town in Maine and that my family are still living there in peace and quiet, without bombs and shells falling around them? Is there any place in the world like that anymore? It's hard to believe. I know that Ken is somewhere in the Marine Corps, but I have no idea where. And another brother is probably in the service, but [I] have not heard from home since before the war, [and] I cannot be sure where anyone is.

Back in Maine, on May 22, 1942, a headline in the *Bangor Daily News* read "BANGOR NURSE IS KILLED IN ACTION OR HELD PRISONER."[7]

Alice's family was offered a gold-star service flag to be put in the living room window, indicating that a soldier from the household had been killed. Alice's mother would have none of it. She was sure Alice was coming home. In what she called her "war corner," there were pictures of Ken and Alice on the wall, and below these photos stood the Philco radio, with its big dial and rounded top. Mary would sit in her rocking chair, read the paper, and listen to the news.

Later there would be word of Alice on which they could pin their hopes, arriving in letters from several nurses who had been rescued by either submarine or PBY from Corregidor.

Besides members of Alice's family, several people had been searching for some news of Alice. Miss Kathleen Young, superintendent of the nursing program at Eastern Maine General Hospital, was one of these. Miss Young was able to contact Lieutenant Florence MacDonald, who was back in Massachusetts after being rescued from Corregidor. Could she give Alice's family and friends any reassurance that Alice was all right?

The answer was a conditional "yes." "I knew Miss Zwicker in the tunnel. She was grand and so jolly! She was quite well when I left."

Lieutenant Ann Bernatitus,[8] who had been evacuated from Corregidor along with eleven other nurses by the submarine,[9] wrote with assurance to Alice's mother. Alice and Ann had been together since the outbreak of the war, first at St. Scholastica's in Manila, and then at Limay, Little Baguio, and finally, on Corregidor. In those places, they had served together in the operating rooms. Ann wrote:

Please believe me, when I say she was well and looking good and just as happy all day long. She always kept the rest of the crowd in good humor by her singing. She had such a lovely voice. I saw her the night I left Corregidor and she, as all the others, wished us luck and God Speed . . . and don't forget to smile, for I know Alice would want you to.[10]

Only a few could be evacuated from Corregidor, and there were some hard feelings about selection. If Alice harbored such feelings, neither she nor her friends allowed it to show at that moment of parting, even though those left behind knew that their last chance was leaving too.

Some years later, Alice wrote down her recollections of life within the Rock:

May 6, 1942. The place is Corregidor, the "Gibraltar of the Pacific." I don't know whether the sun is shining or not because I have been in the tunnels for nearly a month. And if one is smart one does not venture out for anything. The last group of men who went out to one of the tunnel entrances for a last minute smoke before retiring were picked up in a basket when a Japanese shell from Bataan hit the entrance.[11]

For days the tunnels have been full of gunpowder smoke, and it is difficult to breathe. But the ventilators must remain open if we are to remain alive. We do not know that this is the day of surrender of the Rock. But we do know that it's probable, because last night the Japs made a landing here.[12]

Patients and personnel were restless last night and for the past several days, but today, oddly enough, everyone seems rather calm. Maybe it is the realization that at last this phase of the fighting is nearly over. For months we have done our best with all the odds against us, but this month has been rugged. Once Java and Sumatra fell, the Japs concentrated on Bataan and Corregidor. And after Bataan fell on April ninth, they've poured everything they had on to this place. Bombs, shells, mortars, the works, until it seemed that surely the place will be splintered to bits.[13]

We are told that there [is] 350 feet of rock over us, but in one place there is only about 50 feet, and I have often wondered where that 50 feet is! Even during a thunderstorm the repercussion in the tunnels is bad. Can you imagine what it has been like with constant bombardment for over a month?[14] And because it's [Corregidor]—what it is and where it is—it's a perfect target! They never miss hitting something. The casualties have been heavy, and fighting equipment now practically gone. More and more of the patients being admitted are young kids who have simply gone haywire trying to fight bombs and shells without even rifles. Only their bare hands and their guts. But after a while, courage is just not enough. and something gives.

We've known that the Rock would have to go, but when? We know that we must be sacrificed for the present in order to build up an offensive probability in Australia. And so we've held on, even if it would have been easier to surrender. But last night word came that the Japs had made a landing. And why not? What is to stop them? They could have landed before this had they but known it!

Anyhow, last night everyone was rather jittery. Guess we expected the Japs to take over then and behead us all. But apart from knowing that they had made a landing, we, in the hospital tunnels, have heard no more. The hospital tunnels are somewhat removed from the main tunnel by a maze of passageways, so we have no idea what's going on, and no one has come back to give us word. The only thing that I wonder about is whether the Japs will use gas in the tunnels. To be trapped here with gas would be dying the hard way, and no mistake, so all of us keep our gas masks within easy reach at all times.

Though General Wainwright surrendered to the Japs at noon, we hear nothing of it until later in the day. No word comes back to us in the hospital lateral.[15] But, of course, that is not strange. Once the Japs took over, nobody was permitted back here, and we did not see the Japs that day at all. When we do hear that the Rock has fallen at last, most of us feel only relief that it is over—at least for a while.

Supplies of all kinds are nearly gone. Water, soap, and bare essentials are things of the past. Corregidor generated her own electricity, but much of her water supply was brought from Bataan on barges. Once the Japs began their offensive, we were cut off from water, and our electric unit has long since been out of commission because of the Jap bombing. Light in the tunnels is provided by batteries.

Conditions in the tunnel had become desperate. Everyone did what they could. Alice encountered Marine Sergeant Harry F. Morris among the wounded, stumbling into the tunnel. He was blinded by his own blood from a grotesque head wound. Her first aid saved his left eye.

The men here on this fortress have fought so hard. They are hungry and worn out, and so are the rest of us. At which point I will be mighty glad to hear that it is over, at least for a while. Even all the rumors of what the Japs may do to us, and especially the women, mean little or nothing to me at present. Just end this awful destruction and find help for these patients who need the barest essentials so badly. Even a bath would help. . . .

We do not see the Japs until the following day, when they made an inspection of the hospital laterals. And then we had to stand with our backs to them, which suited us all, too! Actually it was a quiet time. We were permitted to go about our work and to go out and sit in the sun by the tunnel entrances, with Jap guards, and it seemed good to get out again. But Corregidor was demolished, and with the fall of the "impregnable Rock" and the entire Philippines, we're now in enemy hands.[16]

One of the first acts of the victors was to take ten nurses outside the tunnel entrance for a photograph, which evidently was to be used as proof that these women were being well cared for. Outside, the gruesome lay wherever one looked. The Allied dead had not been buried, and the bodies lay bloated and covered with flies.[17]

Whatever good intentions the Japanese had toward the nurses, they seemed perplexed by the very idea of female prisoners of war. There was curiosity as well. The nurses felt like creatures in a zoo; they were something to be stared at. The nurses slept in their clothes, for they never knew when there would be the tramp of boots and another visit or "inspection."

After the newness wore off, the Japanese soldiers began taking anything of value that the nurses had not successfully hidden away. There were slaps, and they were threatened with bayonet points, but no rape, and only one incident of a nurse being physically attacked. One reason that the nurses were not molested was Chief Nurse Gladys "Ann" Mealor's insistence that they keep closely grouped, with someone on watch at all times. She realized the power of the herd.

The patient number rapidly dropped to four hundred, as the Japanese ordered men from their sickbeds to the prisoner pens. Still, the nurses were kept in the tunnels. They were a sorry sight when they finally emerged, many sick, and nearly all marred by skin infections from the humid, festering environment. By June 25, the entire hospital and medical staff had taken up quarters in the bombed-out ruins of Fort Mills Hospital on Topside. There was no roof, just glorious sky, and soon, all around, pails of gardenias in full bloom placed there by the nurses.

The stay at Fort Mills was short. On July 2, it was announced that medical staff and patients would be taken to Manila. The tramp steamer *Lima Maru*, a calico of rust and old paint, was anchored off what had once been Corregidor's south pier. It was a hot, sticky day. The nurses sat in the sun onshore while the Japanese took their time getting organized. Finally, the nurses were taken out to this ship in small boats. At the *Lima Maru*, they were faced with a rope ladder by which they were expected to climb aboard.

Madeline Ullom had dengue fever and a temperature of 104. The world began to swim around her as she neared the top of the ladder; she thought of sharks in the harbor and made a last effort.

Alice was also weak. One wonders if she looked straight ahead at the riveted plates in the ship's hull as she pulled herself upward. Did she pretend she was climbing up to the tree house in Brownville, where tangy root beer, cold from the spring, awaited her?

The square in Brownville; the Briggs Block is located in the upper right. (Brownville Historical Society)

The house on Pleasant Street that the Zwicker children called home. (Zwicker Family Collection)

Mary Zwicker and her children dressed in their Sunday best. Catherine stands before her mother, Alice to the left, little Kenneth in the middle, and Helena on the right. The Congregational Church is in the background. (Zwicker Family Collection)

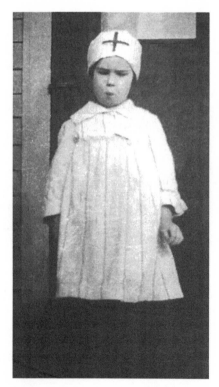

Being a nurse is serious business; little Alice in her homemade nursing costume. (Zwicker Family Collection)

Alice's graduation photo.
(Zwicker Family Collection)

Handsome Fred Newell
in his Annapolis whites.
(Zwicker Family Collection)

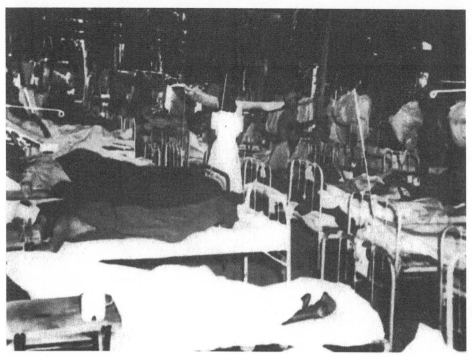

Though poor in quality, this photo shows the crowded wards of Hospital No. 1 on Bataan. (U.S. Army Signal Corps)

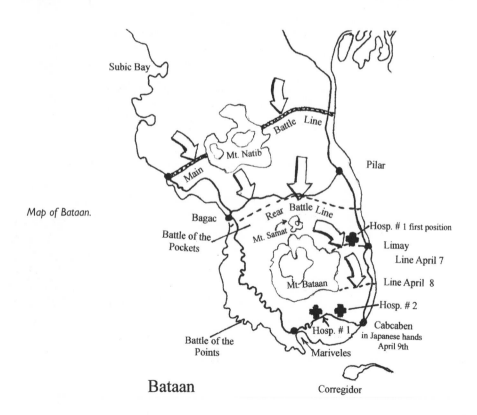

Map of Bataan.

Subic Bay

Battle Line

Mt. Natib

Main

Pilar

Bagac

Rear Battle Line

Mt. Samat

Battle of the Pockets

Hosp. # 1 first position

Limay

Line April 7

Mt. Bataan

Line April 8

Hosp. # 2

Hosp. # 1

Cabcaben
in Japanese hands
April 9th

Battle of the Points

Mariveles

Bataan

Corregidor

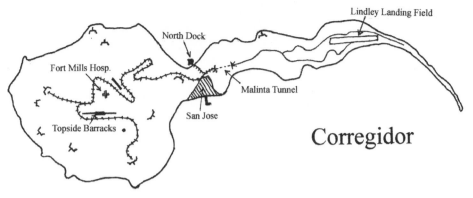

Map of Corregidor.

Christmas, 1945. The family is finally together again for the holidays. Despite the happiness of the occasion and the joy of the war being over, the haunted eyes of the veterans in the back row (Alice is second from left) reveal their experiences are not so easily overcome. (Zwicker Family Collection)

Sisters, tested and true: nurses on the beach at Leyte. Left to right: Helen Cassiani, Anne Wurtz, Alice, Letha McHale, Catherine Acorn, and Rita Palmer. (Zwicker Family Collection)

Alice and her sister nurses became celebrated figures upon their return. Here Alice poses with a soldier she met in the Philippines. (Zwicker Family Collection)

A radiant Alice steps from the plane in New York City. Later, during a homecoming program, Alice was presented with this photo, provided by the postmaster of New York City. (Zwicker Family Collection)

Alice reunited with her mother and father. (Bangor Daily News)

Alice addressing the Red Cross rally in Bangor. (Bangor Daily News)

Ken and Marilyn's wedding party at the Latin Quarter in New York. Left to right: Alice, Don Caswell (an admiring friend from Brownville), Ken, and Marilyn. The stuffed animals were surprise guests. (Zwicker Family Collection)

Alice's wedding: A newly united Mr. and Mrs. Robert Dameron. (Zwicker Family Collection)

A smile from Alice, recuperating at the Veterans' Hospital in Rutland, Massachusetts, after her pneumonectomy. (Zwicker Family Collection)

Alice's beloved camp at Bonny Eagle Lake in Maine. (Zwicker Family Collection)

Portrait of Alice in her captain's uniform. (Zwicker Family Collection)

9

SANTO TOMAS

The nurses could never be sure how their captors would treat them in any new situation.

As the *Lima Maru* lumbered her way toward Manila, the Japanese captain invited the nurses to tea. He was an urbane young man, dressed in his whites and anxious to talk. He, too, would be glad to get back home, he told the nurses, who were in no mood for condescending prattle. Their patients and countrymen were down below, crowded into the ship's steaming hold, and doubtless in a state of neglect.[1]

There won't be much left of Japan when we get through, they told the captain.

"Japan?" he answered, "Hell, I'm not talking about Japan; I'm talking about Pasadena!"

Just before the war, he had gone back to Japan to visit relatives and had been forced into the Imperial Navy. In a sense he, too, was a prisoner. Wars leave one wondering about such generalized terms as "the Japanese." Years later, Alice and her sister nurses would have to negotiate between the hatred they felt for those who had cruelly destroyed so much and the memory of those among their enemies who had shown instances of kindness arising from a common humanity.

What was certain was that a well-equipped Japanese army led by an often ruthless and regimented tribe of warriors had, in an amazingly short period of time, swept the Pacific Islands and much of the Far East. Now the victorious Japanese were faced with the huge task of administrating their "new world order."

What to do with the captured nurses would have been relatively unimportant in their overall scheme of things had it not been for world opinion. How was the Imperial government to deal with this extraordinary situation of women in uniform? More than that, what were they to do with women officers? They could not exchange them. They had to appear to be treating these nurses well, for the Japanese world image had been tarnished enough with all of the reported atrocities. The best solution was to contain these nurses in a civil internment camp where they would be hidden away amid the other aliens.

—⁓—

Once spoken of as the "Pearl of the Orient," Manila was now desolate, with battered hulks in the harbor and blackened ruins along the waterfront. The sick and wounded from Corregidor were unloaded, and the doctors and orderlies were herded into line.

The nurses began to join the queue. They had been told by the Japanese that they would be staying with their patients, and together would be going to a school in Paranaque that had been outfitted as a hospital. Alice thought it was too good to be true, but just maybe their lot was changing. And then, motioning with their bayonet points, the soldiers moved the fifty-four nurses to three trucks, each with waiting guards. They made slow progress through the wreckage of the city.

Nurse Madeline Ullom knew this part of Manila. They were not heading for Paranaque.

"This is not the way to Paranaque. It's that road up there," Madeline told the Japanese driver. She felt a bayonet point touch her back and decided to keep still.[2]

In the midst of this nightmare that engulfed them, they were being separated once again from their patients, torn from those who had become their reason for being.

Years later, Alice sent a photo of Corregidor veterans to her young friend, Terry Myers. "Look at these men," Alice wrote. "They made their own peg legs. This is what we left behind us. So you wonder why we were so bitter."

They crossed the Pasig River and headed generally northeast down Calle España (España Boulevard). The cavalcade slowed; on the left was a long, twelve-foot-high wall of stone and concrete with a section of spiked-iron fence and gate at its center. Japanese guards swung open the gate, and with the crunch of changing gears, the trucks turned and passed through.

Behind the wall was the sixty-acre enclave that had been the campus of an old school, Santo Tomas, founded by the Dominicans in 1611, and declared a public university by Pope Innocent XI seventy years later. When the Angels of Bataan arrived, Santo Tomas was a Japanese camp for civil internees. It would be the nurses' crowded, restricted, and troubled world for the next three years.

During those prewar weeks in Manila—those halcyon days of dinners, dates, and dances—Alice probably had no knowledge that the American Emergency Committee existed. Formed in January of 1941,[3] this group of prominent Americans, largely from Manila's corporate community, was united in a shared concern over the growing Japanese threat to the peace and prosperity of the Philippines. Their purpose was to counteract the inertia that seemed so prevalent despite the handwriting on the wall.

The members of the committee established air raid shelters and evacuation centers. They encouraged the wives and children of U.S. citizens to return home. At the outbreak of war, the committee had approached the university officials at Santo Tomas, suggesting that its campus might be used to house internees. When war came, the resulting agreement was presented to the commander of the occupying Japanese forces.[4]

For the invaders—the "foreign nationals," of whom Manila had a large array—presented more of a nuisance than a danger. The Japanese would round up these people and contain them, but they had no intention of feeding them. For them, a Japanese-controlled, internee-run camp was a welcome solution.

What resulted at Santo Tomas was a community by committee controlled by the Japanese Bureau of External Affairs and led by an amazing group of American and British internees, many of whom had been executives of large corporations. Among these leaders were those with experience gained in serving on the American Emergency Committee.

In the tropical heat of that late afternoon, the trucks crept up the avenue toward the main building of the university. The building had been constructed to impress: a large, three-story, ornamental structure with a square clock tower, topped with a cupola and a white cross. Though as yet untouched by shells or bombs, the building seemed a "wreck of paradise," a thing mislaid in a world where education and higher religious intentions no longer had a place.

Alerted by the authorities that a "special group of prisoners was arriving,"[5] internees had crowded into the open space before the main building and gathered along the sides of the drive. When word spread of the newcomers' identity, the internees shouted urgent questions concerning missing people, and about what had truly happened to the Allied defenders. The order was given that there would be no communication, and the guards quickly threatened internees and new prisoners alike.

At first, the nurses protested being separated from their patients by refusing to get off the trucks. With their rifles and ubiquitous bayonets, the Japanese guards indicated that they had no patience for foolishness.[6] They hurried the nurses into a small room in the main building. There was food waiting: rice, pineapple, and something the nurses had not tasted for a long while—shreds of meat. Then the guards searched the nurses' meager baggage[7] and did their own questioning. It was a slow process.

One by one the nurses were allowed to go down the hallway to a toilet. On these trips, the nurses were able to share whispered bits of conversation with waiting internees. To the nurses, news of the Battle of Midway was a tonic. In response to Alice's questions about Lieutenant Fred Newell, there was no news.

The Japanese had a practice of keeping new prisoners isolated. When the searching of their belongings was finished, the nurses were reloaded onto the trucks and driven to a side gate in Santo Tomas's northeast wall, then across a street and into a much smaller enclosure that boxed in the convent of Santa Catalina. There were nuns still occupying the first floor of the convent building, so the nurses were herded to the second floor. They were told that there would be no communication with the internees in Santo Tomas, or with the nuns downstairs. The arrangements were simple: They would be fed from the main camp, and they would be allowed out in the yard for two hours a day.

And so they were left.

The nurses from Bataan and Corregidor had arrived in a sorry state of health and spirits. What they needed, and what the Japanese unintentionally had given them, was a chance to sleep, to heal each other, and to bond more intimately into a sisterhood. The fittest of their number nursed those with dysentery, malaria, and a host of other infections that left them too sick to work. Together, those well enough did what they had been taught to do: They cleaned, organized the assortments of cots, and marshaled what resources they had. Conditions at Santa Catalina, though crowded and contained, were the best the nurses had seen for months. In the evening, when the sunset made a glory in the sky, a group of the "girls" would sit on the windowsills and sing old songs. Alice, who was still suffering from the effects of dengue fever, benefited from the healing atmosphere.

On August 6, 1942, Alice turned twenty-six. Resources were few at Santa Catalina; still, seven of Alice's closest friends made her a birthday card tied together with a bit of ribbon and string. Somewhere her friends had found and cut out a silhouette of a dancer with a lovely arch of back and delicate extension of fingers. They pasted that picture on the front of their homemade card, while inside, beside their names, was a cut-out stanza from Sara Teasdale's poem, "Barter," which contained these lines: "Spend all you have for loveliness / Buy it and never count the cost."

Those signing the card included Minneapolis-born Phyllis Arnold, who had sailed with Alice on the *Holbrook,* and who had become renowned when she captured the hated monkey, "Tojo," that had ravaged the nursing lateral in Malinta Tunnel; Helen Cassiani (Cassie), a surgical nurse from Bridgewater, Massachusetts, who has already been mentioned as the first nurse to volunteer to help at Stotsenberg Hospital when the bombs came smashing down; Alice Hahn, whom Alice listed as one of the people she wanted to remember; and Mildred (Millie) Dalton from Jefferson, Georgia, who was to become Alice's closest friend at Santo Tomas.[8]

In 2013, Millie was the last surviving Angel of Bataan, at the age of ninety-eight. In 2011, she wrote: "Alice was a wonderful person. She befriended so many people in Santo Tomas. . . . I love her still."[9]

A few weeks later, the nurses were moved again. As the population in Santo Tomas rose to over three thousand, the subcommittee on medicine[10] recommended that Santa Catalina be transformed into a hospital. On August 28, 1942, the nurses were transferred from their improvised quarters in the convent to even more cramped quarters behind the main building on the Santo Tomas campus. When they were finally housed in the main building, space per nurse was limited to six feet by forty inches.

As for privacy, there was none. Some wit posted a sign in the shower area that read, "If you want privacy, shut your eyes." The women waited in line for one of the few toilets, a washstand, or a turn at the old bathtub in the yard, where the nurses washed their hair. They also had a shuffling wait in the long food lines. Waiting in line became a way of life.[11]

For a while, the Red Cross had undertaken the feeding of the internees; however, by the time the nurses were removed from Santa Catalina, Red Cross funds had been depleted, and starvation was averted by the Camp Executive Committee's persistent negotiation with the Japanese and the help of the camp commandant, Mr. Tsurumi. Finally, it was agreed that an allotment would be given by the Japanese for food and utilities. It was meager, but it staved off disaster, ensuring the survival of the many poorer internees, including Alice and her sister nurses. To supplement the survival diet provided, those internees who had money could shop at the markets that the Japanese allowed within the camp for the first two years.[12]

Fundamental to the well-being of the internees and the operation of the camp was the requirement that all of the able internees would work, even if only a few hours a day (the number of hours required varied by age groups). Frederic Stevens describes a general manager of a large electric company solemnly handing out the allotment of four sheets of toilet paper to each person as he or she stood in line for the facilities. There was something for everyone to do.

Captain Maude Davison, ranking officer among the nurses, was anxious to get her women working. She wasn't pleased with their first assignments, which involved cleaning the kitchen and toilets. Her nurses were professional medical staff, and Davison pushed the Medical Committee to have them given proper medical tasks.

Professional recognition was crucial, but so, too, was keeping the nurses together as a working unit of the Army Medical Corps. It was not surprising that Captain Davison could be "domineering and antagonistic."[13] Both she and her second in command, Josie Nesbit, were worried. They were aware that in this new situation, their nurses were subject to divisive influences and demoralizing conditions.

As far as the nurses' relationships with men, there was little Captain Davison could do. Nurse Alice Hahn remembered: "We were at an age where we pretty soon formed alliances with men. We had friendships pretty much the same way we would in normal life, the normal boy and girl relationships, what you would expect. I met my husband in prison camp."[14]

For Alice, there was a deep sense of personal aloneness, despite the close friendships she had formed with a number of the women. Some years later, when Alice filled out a personal service record booklet that

someone had given her, she wrote "No *him*!!" in the blank following
the prompt, "Visits to him." One assumes she meant that special, one
and only "him," for Alice soon found male friends among internees, and
close friends, too.

With the green ink she liked to use, she made a list of the people she
wanted to remember in her notebook, and when she discovered that her
date from the Manila days, Bob Dameron, was among the internees at
Santo Tomas, she added to her list Dameron's California address and
that of his parents. As the months dragged into years behind the prison
walls, their friendship became a romance.

She copied the following lines from "Sweet Heartache" into her
notebook:

> I'm glad you're back, sweet heartache,
> It means I'm in love again
> Sweet kisses that lips as eager as mine
> Will add to my sweet heartache.

Then she added after this quote, "Boy—just once again."

While Captain Davison's problems with developing alliances between men and nurses were inevitable, there was one issue about
which she could do something. The nurses required spending money
to buy the food they so badly needed from the markets (duck eggs, carabao milk, and fruit). Beyond the crucial problem of diet and buying
extra food, some discretionary money was also important for morale.
Without it, one could not enjoy an occasional extravagance, such as
going to the hairdressing "salon" that some enterprising internees had
established within the camp. Without a little money, that all-important
semblance of normalcy would be lost, and then, worst of all possibilities, the confinement, crowding, and privation might cause younger
nurses to sell their services. That specter was what Davison and Nesbit
feared the most.

There was money to be borrowed. Some internees had brought
considerable amounts of money into the camp, while others retained

connections with the companies that had employed them, and could arrange for the transfer of funds. The nurses with their military pay accumulating at home were good risks for small loans. These loans weren't free, but the interest would not start until after the war was over.

Alice kept a careful record of the money she borrowed in a small notebook. The amounts entered are more often in pesos than in dollars. She borrowed one hundred pesos from a Richard McGarth, more from her friend Bob Dameron, and $36.50 from a Major Davidson. One name in the notebook's list was Carroll Grinnell. In peacetime, Grinnell had managed General Electric's interests in the Far East. At Santo Tomas, he was chair of the Internee Administration Committee, which handled the Japanese allotment to the internees. He and three other camp leaders were arrested shortly before the liberation of Santo Tomas, and, in February of 1945, their beheaded bodies were found buried in Manila. No one seemed to know why they were murdered.

In all, Alice borrowed $630. She paid it all back, including the money she owed Carroll Grinnell. That sum was sent to his company. It should be noted that, some years later, the U.S. government refunded Alice and the other nurses for the money they had paid to their Santo Tomas creditors.

One way or another, the nurses got along during those first two years as internees. The camp was providing two rather poor meals a day. Frances Nash, one of Alice's roommates, remarked that the cornmeal mush regularly served tasted "like wallpaper paste." There were sometimes bits of carabao meat, but often there was more protein in the weevils. Alice and six other nurses pooled their resources to have a table built, which they kept in the hallway. The nurses bought fruit and vegetables and took turns making the salads that were their noonday lunch.[15] This gathering around the table had both dietary and social benefits.

Those internees who had more substantial sums of money escaped the noise and crowding by building a shanty or having it built for them. The number of shanties grew to over six hundred, filling all the available spaces on the old campus. The clumped "villages" were given fanciful names: Foggy Bottom, Over Yonder, and, prosaically, Shantytown. The latter was a pleasant place in the dry season.[16] The structures themselves varied from makeshift shacks to nipa cottages with tar-paper or thatched roofs, sawali sides, and bamboo floors.

The Japanese commandant struggled with regulating this shanty world. Shanties had to be constructed with two open sides, supposedly exposing what was going on within. At first they could be occupied only during daytime hours; then, because of the need for housing of some kind, husbands were allowed to sleep in the shanties. When wives were allowed to follow their husbands in February 1944, there was a large increase in pregnancies.

As a guest, Alice went as often as she could to a shanty where there was a small Victrola. Though dancing was forbidden except under authorized conditions, there were times when she dared to dance; and then, according to several friends, she was in "seventh heaven." Alice herself often said that she "would rather dance than eat." She would learn that, when one is starving, eating becomes an all-consuming need. There was truth, however, in what Alice had said. She never lost her love of dancing, and music remained a passion. One of her favorite topics of conversation was dance records she was going to get when the war was over. She often wondered what the latest dance hits were.

Christmas 1942 was a marvelous improvement over the Christmas of a year before, when the nurses had faced war on Bataan. Alice claimed that she could not sew a stitch, but she managed to help in the making of rag dolls and other presents for the children in the camp. The nurses made gifts for each other as well, and on Christmas Day they all gathered around a long table on the grounds behind their quarters for a hoarded holiday dinner.

As intended, it was a season of giving. A group of army engineers who were prison workers at Malinta Tunnel found a cache of money hidden in a tunnel wall and managed to send it as a gift to the nurses. In addition to this unexpected generosity, and for the first and only time during their internment, Red Cross packages were allowed to reach the internees.[17] There was also a package for Alice from home—the only one she would ever receive.

Alice wrote her thanks on a card supplied by the Imperial Japanese Army. The message was limited to twenty-five words. Alice wrote: "Received package you sent. It was swell. Everything I needed. Glad to know you are all well. Would sure like seeing you. Love, Alice."

Adding to the color and generosity of the season was a gift of fruitcake and turkey from another interesting benefactor. The Japanese allowed Ida Haentsche Hube of Manila unusual freedom—evidently because she had married a German, and it was said that she had once admired Hitler. She had been in Manila for some years, working as a contract nurse for the U.S. Army, and knew Maude Davison and Josephine Nesbit. This was the connection that first brought her to the gate of Santo Tomas, driven in a black limousine. She continued to bring gifts, sometimes in a procession of grocery carts followed by the shining car. Standing in their worn housedresses behind the iron rods of the gate, the nurses enjoyed Ida's arrival and her final check of the carts. She was a flamboyantly elegant figure, wearing long white gloves and walking under a lace parasol.[18]

It was a good Christmas, despite the lack of snow and the larger fact that they were all away from home. One of Alice's favorite poems was "Snow-Bound" by John Greenleaf Whittier. Like Whittier, she remembered how the winter storms had closed them in as a family, together around the stove. And when the storm was over, her father, like the one in the poem, would call them out to shovel in a transformed world:

> Around the glistening wonder bent
> The blue wall of the Firmament
> No cloud above, no earth below,
> A universe of sky and snow!

Alice thought often of home as the days became weeks, and the weeks, years. More and more she thought of her mother.

In the spring of 1942, Alice managed to send another message home. It traveled by way of the island of Cebu, bringing long-distance hope to her family.

Still, no one was sure that Alice had survived Corregidor. In what she called the "war corner" of her sitting room, Mary sat straight in her rocker as she talked to a reporter from the *Bangor Daily News*. Alice had told her mother not to worry about her as long as part of her military pay was sent home. When those checks had stopped arriving at the Brownville post office, Mary had come home and begun to clean the house from top to bottom. She had to do something.

Still, there was never a moment when she was not sure that Alice was coming home.

"Sometimes," Mary told the reporter, "when I get to thinking that the Japanese might abuse my girl, I go into a dark room to think; but you know, every time such thoughts fade away, and I can see only the sunshine."

On August 6, 1943, Mary wrote a message in the birthday card she had picked out for Alice. The card featured a vivacious young lady putting candles on a cake. The curvy young figure was dressed in a puffy cook's cap, a party dress, and red heels that tied around the ankles with bows. Perhaps the girl on the card reminded her mother of Alice. She wrote: "You are always in my mind. I hope this time next year you will be home. God bless my child and send her home. Heaps of love, Ma."

Not knowing where to mail the card, Mary tucked it away with the other unsent cards and messages she had written to Alice.

Alice's brother Kenneth had joined the marines shortly after word came that his sister was missing in action. He told his brother Eli that he intended to find Alice. The marines had offered him a clerical job—Ken was skilled with a typewriter—but he had said, "I can't shoot Japs with a typewriter." He would not be home for Christmas, Mary informed the reporter: "He is in the Pacific," and then she added, speaking of both Alice and Ken, "God will take care of them."[19]

James was away from his wife, working in the Naval Yard at Portsmouth, New Hampshire. Mary kept her vigil alone in the rambling house on Pleasant Street, and treasured her momentary visions of sunshine.

Behind the high encircling wall of Santo Tomas, Alice also had her own moments of sunshine. She spent a day and into the evening in the

Father's Garden, in the company of internee Bill Rivers. At the close of their day together, they chose a page in a liturgical booklet they had acquired. Both signed and dated the page: April 26, 1943. Bill added a note: "A wonderful day." Alice kept the booklet as a memento.[20]

Resilience was the great human victory among the nurses at Santo Tomas—their determination not to be broken, to keep alert and focused, to keep as physically fit as possible, and to do their job.

For Alice, reading, which had always been important to her, now became a blessing. She had to wait her turn for A. J. Cronin's *The Keys of the Kingdom*, but there was much else to choose from in the college library now enriched by books donated by many of the internees. Alice kept a list of the books she read during the first years of her imprisonment. There were 204, along with forty more that she did not finish.[21]

It is an eclectic list: a satire by John Marquand (Alice notes that satire is the cause of her own downfall); *Disputed Passages* by Lloyd Douglass, which Alice rates as excellent; and loads of mysteries by Ellery Queen, Erle Stanley Gardner, and Agatha Christie. The list also includes *Etiquette* by Emily Post, which she laid down before it was completely read; and *The Eagles Gather* by Taylor Caldwell, which Alice rates with another "excellent."[22] There is a sprinkle of classics in her book list, including *Kitty Foyle* by Christopher Morley, Willa Cather's *The Professor's House*, and *Pride and Prejudice* by Jane Austen.

Alice used some of the books she read as textbooks. One of these was on Africa, a topic she had always found interesting. There was a fairly extensive glossary of African words in that volume, which she painstakingly copied, along with pronunciations, into one of her notebooks.

Associated with Alice's reading was her practice of making collections of quotes, aphorisms, poems, course notes, and a record of her own decreasing physical measurements. Three of Alice's notebooks from the Santo Tomas era survive: Two are copybooks originally produced by the Philippine Bureau of Education, and the other, a homemade booklet tied with an old shoelace.[23]

The quotations are culled from magazines and newspapers such as *Harper's*, *Reader's Digest*, and Philadelphia's *Inquirer*. Some are merely sharp and fun: "So pleased to meet you, Miss Guilder. My husband has told me so little about you." Or, "I guess you could call us friends; we have the same enemies." Some must have seemed immediately close to Alice's present situation: "It is good to lie in bed and let sleep's drowsy wind blow out the candles of thought." Some quotes stayed in her mind; Alice later marked them with a cross:

> We must be willing to pay a price for freedom, for no price that is ever asked is half the cost of doing without it.

> Make it a rule of life never to regret and never to look back. Regret is an appalling waste of energy. You can't build on it, it is only good for wallowing in.

There is a page of toasts:

> Here's to Eve, the mother of the race,
> She wore a fig leaf in the proper place.
> Here's to Adam, the father of us all,
> He was "Johnny on the spot" when leaves began to fall.

There is another page with drink recipes, followed by several pages of rollicking ditties, some of which are suggestive:

> I'm tired of whiskey,
> I'm tired of gin,
> I'm tired of virtue,
> I'm tired of sin.
> I'm tired of the big apple
> And I'm tired of truckin'
> And after last night—gosh, am I tired!!

Some of Alice's quoted "verses" were garnered from the men she had nursed. Major Phillip Breese, "Ward III Tunnel—Corregidor," contributed lines on a Chinese impression of an American cocktail.

Alice listed her fourteen favorite poems. They are quite different from those just mentioned. They are poems that those fortunate enough to be educated in New England schools often memorized, written by stalwart poets such as Wordsworth, Whittier, and Longfellow. Some of her favorite poems Alice copied into her notebook, including "If" by Rudyard Kipling and Sam Walter Foss's "The House by the Side of the Road," which often repeats, "But let me live in a house by the side of the road, and be a friend to man."

Her interests were never boxed in. She especially liked a long poem by Don Blanding titled "Vagabond House."[24] There was the spell of the Pacific Islands in Blanding's poetry, and something more that resonated with Alice. It had to do with finding oneself:

> When I have a house—as I sometime may—
> I'll suit my fancy in every way.
>
> I told of the things I chose myself
> To grace my house—those priceless things
> That an hour of idle dreaming brings.
>
> And the house you build of fragile stuff
> Is the same as mine, if we dream enough.

Alice's house would be a long time in the building.

There was a place for the teacher's name on the covers of the copybooks that Alice used. On one, Alice filled in this space with "Myself."[25] There are few personal reflections in these notebooks, and no notes on current events. Instead, one finds lists of word meanings and of words often mispronounced. These and other entries are the record of one endeavoring not to forget, and to keep preoccupied through improvement of skills.

Unlike many of the nurses, Alice had never played bridge. She learned the rudiments of shuffling cards with her pals while the smell of hibiscus wafted through the second-floor windows of Santa Catalina, but she went on to diligently learn the rules and study the strategies of the game. She filled sixteen notebook pages with notes and annotations on probabilities, situations, and the recommended best plays. Assisting her endeavors was a course in bridge offered through the internee-run adult education program.

As a result of the internees' resilient efforts, many opportunities existed within the camp. There was an extensive sports program; drama flourished with the creation of the "Theater under the Stars"; and there was a wide variety of courses in the multifaceted adult education programs. The nurses found these endeavors in place when they arrived at the camp and eagerly participated.

Contending with the chronic ailments she had picked up on Bataan and Corregidor, as well as night duty, hindered Alice's involvement in courses offered by the Education Committee. She did take a Carnegie-type course on "How to Win Friends and Influence People." One of the doctors among the internees taught a rather technical course in urology, and Alice took that as well.

As far as her strength allowed, Alice also participated in sports. Baseball and softball thrived, with a number of teams and league activities. The Baseball Committee published a booklet called *Baseball Program and Schedule*, and on the page of "ads" Alice has a box declaring her allegiance for one of the Santo Tomas teams: "The Boston Braves are near my heart."

But watching and cheering were not enough. Alice and other athletic women wanted to play. Under Lieutenant Helen "Cassie" Cassiani's and Alice's leadership, the "STIC Nurses" team joined with three other teams to form the Women's Softball League. Cassie's brother had played in the minor leagues, and Cassie knew how to field a ball and throw a runner out at first base—or any other base, as the situation demanded. Like many of the other nurses on this team, Alice had grown up with brothers and neighborhood ball games where girls, if not entirely welcome, were necessary. The team was no pushover, but they were outclassed by the Bureau of Education Team, composed of schoolgirls who had both skill and youth on their side.

A leader of this younger team was fourteen-year-old Terry Myers. She was dark-haired and vivacious and had a remarkable resemblance to Cassie—so much so that the nurses called her "Little Cassie." The nurses took Terry's story to heart. She and her brother had been left in Manila with their father while her mother and two younger siblings

went to the United States on a visit. The two older children were supposed to join their mother when school closed for Christmas, but the
Japanese came first. Terry's father had decided to join a guerrilla group,
and had left Terry and her brother with their grandparents. The Japanese rounded up the grandparents and children and took them to Santo
Tomas, and then, because of crowding and their age, the grandparents
were dismissed from the camp, leaving the children behind.

Terry's relationship with the nurses grew. She sent a homemade
Christmas card to Alice in 1943, on which she wrote: "To Alice (Flash),
One of the *Best*." Later, during the hard last days in the internment
camp, Terry worked as a helper in the surgical section of the hospital.
She vowed that she would become a nurse and go to the training school
in Bangor from which Alice had graduated.

The *Baseball Program and Schedule* featured a delightful cartoon on
its front cover. The look on the batter's face in this drawing as the ball
whistles past and the empire yells "Strike!" is wonderfully executed.
That cartoon is an example of the talent that abounded in so many areas
within the eclectic community of internees.

From the very beginning, artistic, musical, and dramatic elements
were well represented in the camp. The nurses missed the first performances produced by the Entertainment Committee, presented from
a stage of planks mounted on soap boxes.[26] However, they were very
much part of the action when the "Little Theater under the Stars" came
into being on January 29, 1943. Starting with vaudeville and quiz shows,
complete with prizes such as tubes of toothpaste, the offerings became
increasingly sophisticated, including *The Man Who Came to Dinner* and
Arsenic and Old Lace.

Music was also varied. A chorus with a hundred voices sang from
Handel's *Messiah* for Christmas 1943. Nearly every night there was popular music, and often the younger crowd of internees would gather on the
basketball court for impromptu dancing while the Japanese guards kept
blowing their whistles.[27] According to Alice's recollection, the Japanese
officials allowed twelve formal dances. "I never missed one," Alice said.
That was an achievement, considering Alice's up-and-down health.

Not even the monsoon season vanquished the Entertainment Committee. When the rains and mud came, they shifted their efforts from outside opportunities to creating a radio-type programming using the camp's loudspeaker system.

All of this emphasis on activity and entertainment was a conscious attempt to find meaning and maintain, as one internee leader phrased it, "cheerfulness and happiness in [the] midst of privation."[28] Yet no matter what was attempted or accomplished, Santo Tomas was, in reality, a restrictive internment camp. At first, it was a matter of rules, such as the requirement that all internees bow upon meeting any Japanese. Alice often told how, when a group of nurses met a guard or official, they would bow one at a time, keeping their captors bobbing in return. "They never caught on," Alice would laughingly add. "Humor is one thing they could not take out of us Americans. . . . Americans stymied them; they couldn't get us down."[29]

Rules were instituted, and then enforcement gradually waned, but the facts of daily life were immutable. There were five showers for two hundred women in the main building. The quantity of bedbugs seemed infinite. Frederic Stevens commented that "bedbugs ran close to first for public enemy number one." But more serious than bedbugs was the lack of food. Sixty acres filled with buildings, shanties, and over four thousand people become a very small world in which to spend three years, especially when the last year was one of famine and a slow descent into hell.

Cinderella was performed for the children as part of the celebration of Christmas 1943. Alice added to the festivities by jiving up seasonal songs on the piano, and the usual dolls for the little girls and holiday cards for adults were made and distributed. A large crowd of the interns' Filipino friends, associates, and servants came to the gate on Christmas morning with food.[30] Alice and a group of eight nurses shared a can of Spam and manufactured a Christmas pudding with a sprig of a red Filipino berry, much like holly. To top off this creation, they added medical alcohol, which burned blue.[31] Still, beneath all of these Christmas customs and with all the trying to be merry, there permeated the apprehension that the quality of life behind the walls of Santo Tomas was slipping downward.

Alice and Millie Dalton had become very close. People used to ask if they were sisters. They decided to volunteer for night duty in the eighty-bed isolation hospital at the rear of the campus. It meant working on the tuberculosis ward and amid other contagious diseases, but there were advantages. They were both "day sleepers," and working nights would get them a place to sleep in the hospital. They had to sleep together, but that was so much better than the very crowded and noisy dormitory in the main building.

They would lie down after a night's work and talk about home, the people there, and their youth. They talked of berry picking, making blueberry pies, and wearing long coats in the summertime because it was the fashion. Millie described her mother bent over a "rickety sewing machine," making their clothes, and how her mother would send her daughter with eggs to exchange for a spool of thread. It must have been a mile and a half or more to walk.[32] Once, Alice told of the Brownville neighbor who fell totally in love with a young woman. She married someone else, and as she and her new husband rode out of town in a buggy, the stricken neighbor ran past the Zwicker home, yelling, "Come back! Come back!" That story had always been amusing to Alice and her siblings, but now in Santo Tomas, it seemed only terribly poignant.

There was a young Catholic priest serving with them as an orderly. Alice and Millie would tell him that there couldn't be a God, for if there were, surely He would not allow a war like this to happen. The priest's response was simple: He would pray them into the church. Perhaps he spoke prophetically.

As the situation in the city surrounding the camp worsened, prices for additional food from outside rose to exorbitant heights. When the ingredients for a cake cost one hundred dollars, such creations became mere treasured memories. In November of 1943, a typhoon left the campus flooded. Nurses waded waist-deep when going to work at Catalina Hospital. When the waters receded, many of the shanty clusters were left in deep mud. From the dirty waters left by the storm rose harbingers of worsening times.

For Alice and many other internees, poor health had already been a serious problem. Alice's beriberi had returned; she lost weight, suffered from sleeplessness, and had trouble with her eyes. One of the two times that Alice left the Santo Tomas campus took place during this period. She was sent to one of the Manila hospitals for a fluoroscope examination.[33] Vitamin B shots made it possible for Alice to get back on her feet and work her shifts.

Throughout all of this, Alice was careful about her appearance. "Nail polish is a woman's great morale builder," she told a newspaper reporter in 1945. "I never went without it a day." She put her hair up in curlers every night. "I couldn't stand stringy hair. . . . If one commenced to let down one's personal appearance . . . [one] simply went down completely."[34]

The nurses received and made over clothes from the civilian internees, knitted underwear, and made do. They wore housedresses in the morning, and in the afternoon they changed into something better and "fixed-up."[35] With the shortage of clothes, the Japanese relented on their rules on apparel and allowed shorts.

On January 14, 1944, the evening announcements included the following ominous news: The camp was now under the War Prisoner Department of the Imperial Japanese Army. There would be no more payments by the Japanese to the internees' Central Committee for the maintenance of infrastructure or for the sustenance of the civilians and nurses within the camp. The Japanese military would supply the food. They also would supply medical, hospital, and sanitary supplies as they deemed essentially necessary. Apparently, they saw no such need. Speaking of life in Santo Tomas, Alice often used the expression that the Japanese "had the whip hand." The whip had suddenly grown barbs. Whether or not there were white armbands bearing the Japanese characters for "law soldier" among the increased troops sent to Santo Tomas, the influence of the *Kempeitai*—the Japanese equivalent of the Gestapo—was present.

The new military commandant ordered that the camp be sealed off from the outside. The disastrous effect of this order on the internees was immediately obvious. Representatives such as Earl Carroll had been allowed to go out into the surrounding city and purchase food and medical supplies. Secretly they had been able to arrange IOUs with Filipino merchants in exchange for wartime pesos, thus stretching their available money.[36]

As the weeks crept on, surprise inspections and formal roll calls increased. Internees were locked in their rooms at night. Room monitors and internee leaders were called together and told that, from then on, bowing was to be taken seriously. They were told that bowing was an expression of gratitude for what their captors had done for them. Censorship of the internee-run camp radio station also became more strict.[37]

Three British internees went over the wall and were caught. Despite all the efforts of the executive, and even with the sympathetic support of some Japanese camp officials, the escapees were shot. Internee leaders were forced to watch the botched execution and reported that the men were still moaning when they were buried.[38]

Still, news often veiled in some appropriate piece of music got through to the inmates via the loudspeaker system. The Japanese used the same media for their own propaganda. Twice they broadcast that the whole American fleet had been sunk, and once, that sixty-four and a half Japanese planes had returned safely from a mission.[39] The internees got a laugh from the half plane.

As the first months of 1944 passed, it became obvious that the Japanese were preparing to defend Santo Tomas. Foxholes were dug and machine guns set up on the grounds, some directly behind the hospital. Other guns were mounted on the roofs of buildings. To Alice and others watching, it was evident that the campus was being used as a military depot. There were stockpiles of boxes that the internees' interpreter said were labeled "ammunition." Drums of gasoline were piled within fifty feet of the hospital.

In Alice's opinion, the Japanese military was stockpiling military supplies "in an excellent spot to put something they didn't want touched."[40] Alice was told that when representatives of the internees complained about this storage of arms, munitions, and fuel, they were told by the

Japanese officials that the Imperial government had never signed the
Geneva Convention. On the bright side, all of this activity was evidence
that the war was turning against the enemy.

Occasionally the nurses enjoyed little surprise events and nuggets of
happiness. Alice was invited to have breakfast with General Foods executive Howie Hicks and his wife, Jean. It was a wonderful treat. There
was little else in which to take comfort. The available calories per person
had dropped steadily, to six hundred. The deficit was not just in quantity
but in essential nutrients and vitamins.

Nurse Frances Nash saw the results of encroaching starvation: "The
look of hunger is unmistakable. . . . I saw my friends' faces . . . the skin
drawn tight across the bones, their eyes sunken, unnaturally bright and
deeply circled."[41] Alice marked the symptoms in her own deteriorating health, as well as that of others: "The entire camp seemed lifeless."
People could not remember what day it was or what they were expected
to do. Alice found it was all she could do to get out of bed for a four-hour
shift and then go back to bed.

Despite all she had been through in Bataan and on Corregidor, Alice
had begun the Santo Tomas ordeal weighing 135 pounds and with the
reputation of being an athlete. Now she was losing weight and slipping
into illness. For a second time, she was stricken with dengue fever. In
June, she developed bacterial dysentery and was placed for a time in
isolation. In September, her legs were swelling, and, while leaning over,
she collapsed onto the floor. She would lose a total of twenty-three
pounds.[42] Her victory, along with all the nurses at Santo Tomas, was that
she kept serving throughout her ordeal.

Of the nurses' service, historian Elizabeth Norman writes: "Without hospital supplies and medicine, the women could not do much.
. . . They continued to perform basic surgery even after the sterilizer
broke down, and they had to bake their instruments in an oven."[43]
Norman adds that increasingly the only thing the nurses could do was
comfort the dying patients.

Alice estimated that the number of internee deaths each day finally
rose to twelve, out of which ten were due to starvation. Dr. Theodore

Stevenson, an internee working in the camp hospital, was jailed on bread and water (with very little bread) when he refused to remove "starvation" as the cause of death from the death certificates and put down "malnutrition" instead. Alice was incensed. Starvation is not the same as malnutrition, she maintained before the War Crimes Committee. Many, including Alice, wondered if there was not a conscious plan on the part of the Japanese military to eliminate the internees by this very method.

The camp was on the edge of a spreading pestilence and devastation. Desperation overwhelmed the law and order that had been successfully encouraged by the internee government. The internees held tightly to what little belongings they owned, lest they be stolen. Survival became a preoccupation. An internee was trapping sparrows on the roof of the main building; a doctor killed a cat and offered meat to his friends. The Japanese had closed the internees' facility for rat control, and now those rodents began feeding on the piles of dead waiting for mass burial.

There was no doubt now that liberation was on its way—but would it come in time?

10

LIBERATION AND HOME

September 21, 1944, began with the usual routines of survival. The internees of Santo Tomas were accustomed to the sound of Japanese planes and practice dogfights overhead. Then, suddenly, there were planes with white stars in a blue circle diving like silver darts—American planes! Alice was to tell interviewers from the War Crimes Commission, "A beautiful sight I might say. Those boys could fly!"

The guards hustled internees inside. The electricity and gas supply went off. There were two raids that day, and, when Alice and Millie went on duty that night, the sky over Manila was red with the reflected glow of fires. Next morning, the camp disc jockey played "Pennies from Heaven." The bombing raids continued, three or four days a week at first. Alice later reported that she felt "low" on days when the bombers did not come. After January 6, the raids were daily. "We had a bird's-eye view of that dive-bombing of Manila."[1]

The Japanese responded to these raids with antiaircraft barrages. As a result, shrapnel fell upon the Santo Tomas campus. Again, the nurses lived and worked amid the wounded. There were up to three hundred patients to be cared for at a time, many of whom were unable to get out of bed. For many, while their upper bodies were gauntly emaciated, their legs were hugely swollen from beriberi.

The nurses were not spared from this affliction. Eleanor Garen, her legs also swollen from vitamin deficiency, felt she was "walking on the trunks of trees." She had no feeling in her lower arms.[2]

Many of the nurses became incontinent, flooding themselves with urine and embarrassment. Others ceased to menstruate; those who kept their period worried that they could not afford to lose blood.

The weeks dragged into months. Nurse Frances Nash wrote: "There was nothing beautiful in our lives except the sunsets and the moonlight. I would sit at the window for hours dreaming of home."[3] Lieutenant Eunice Young wrote in her diary: "Haven't the energy to write much . . . but we have to keep going to take care of others. Words can never describe how miserable we feel. Will appreciate the simple things of life, if we get out—just never to be hungry again."[4]

On January 2, 1945, the Allies landed on Luzon. Waiting and dug in were over a quarter of a million Japanese. When a "flying column" raid on San Jose managed to free the prisoners from the Bataan Death March, General MacArthur ordered General Vernon Mudge of the First Calvary to use the same knifelike maneuver to free Santo Tomas.

Guided by guerrilla forces and supported by field artillery and marine dive-bombers, the cavalry drove through the enemy and in forty-eight hours was on the outskirts of Manila. The internees heard the increasing sound of the fighting. The guards seemed nervous as they moved around their defenses within the camp. Papers were being burned.

Just after a supper of gruel, eight American dive-bombers buzzed the camp. One of the planes dropped a message tied to a pair of aviation goggles. It read, "Roll out the barrel, Santa Claus is coming." The guards ordered the internees inside.

All the nurses knew that earlier that day the guards had placed barrels under the staircase in the main building. Some brave souls investigated and reported that the barrels were stuffed with something soaked in kerosene. The actual purpose and content of those barrels remains unverified, but for the nurses and internees lying on their crowded cots and locked in the building, the barrels held terror. Many were sure that their captors intended to burn them all.[5]

Fighting all the way, the liberating column crossed the Novaliches Bridge as the Japanese were endeavoring to destroy it and rolled down Quezon Boulevard toward Santo Tomas. All evening of January 3 the sounds of fighting had grown closer to the camp, which lay dark under a strict blackout. Only the very sick slept.

The nurses' rooms on the second floor of the main building overlooked the plaza and provided a view of the campus drive to the main gate. Earlier orders on the loudspeaker had forbidden the internees from standing in the windows, but despite these orders the nurses kept watch. From beyond the campus walls came bursts of machine-gun fire and then the clank of tanks. The fear was expressed that the Japanese were sending tanks to finally destroy them, but others were sure that the gasoline they smelled was American.

And then an M4 Sherman tank came smashing through the gate, followed by another Sherman with the name "Georgia Peach" painted on its side. They came up the avenue and stopped before the main building.[6] Reports differ as to what was called upward to the nurses, but it was too colloquially American to leave any doubt. The internees burst through the locked doors and surrounded the tanks. Liberation had come. The prisoners felt a surge of joy that surmounted their weakness and exhaustion.

Alice and Millie missed this moment. They were on duty in the contagion hospital at the rear of the campus, but were well aware that something momentous was taking place. Suddenly, there were American soldiers outside the hospital—beautiful, huge, robust American men. The nurses had forgotten what health looked like. Millie and Alice danced a brief, spontaneous jig.

Back in the center of the campus, the Americans had run into an obstacle. Some seventy Japanese officers and troops had occupied the Education Building and were holding several hundred internees hostage. The five Japanese officers sent to parley with the Americans walked between crowds of internees and shouts of "Kill them, kill them!" The meeting quickly ended with the shooting of Akibo, a Japanese lieutenant, perhaps the most hated man in Santo Tomas internment camp. He apparently had reached for a suicide grenade in a pouch that hung from his shoulder.[7]

A brief firefight erupted with the Japanese in the Education Building. One American soldier was killed, and three were wounded. There were internees wounded as well. As the Japanese-occupied Education Building blocked the way to Santa Catalina, the principal camp hospital, the wounded were taken to an emergency center set up on the first floor of the main building. There were wounded from the American troops who had fought their way to Santo Tomas as well,[8] and the imprisoned nurses were back in the fight, giving their last reserves of energy.

Negotiations took place with the Japanese commandant and his military troops, and an agreement was reached: The Japanese were allowed to march out of the gate. With that event, Santo Tomas became an important medical and tactical center for the American advance on Manila.

After three years in Santo Tomas, the nurses found they had much to learn. What was penicillin? What did "GI" mean, and what were K-rations? The learning was rapid. When army nurse Rose Rieper noticed that a soldier didn't seem to be eating his K-rations, she asked if she could have them. "Ma'am, if you can eat that, you must be hungry," the soldier answered.[9]

Amid all the extraordinary things that happened in the next few days, someone brought Alice's helmet back to her. It had been issued to her at Fort McKinley on her first morning in the Philippines and then taken by a looting Japanese soldier. Alice had carefully written her name in ink on the inside webbing. Someone had painted a green cross outlined in white on the front of the helmet, but otherwise it looked as it had when she last saw it.[10]

Three days after Santo Tomas was liberated, General Douglas MacArthur came to the camp. Alice later described this event to her brother Ken:

> We knew he was coming, but when I walked out of my quarters in the main building, I was absolutely surprised to find him right there. I just

threw my arms around his waist and said, "Boy, am I glad to see you." Then I suddenly realized you don't do that to a general.

"I'm glad to see you too . . . ," [the general responded].

I remember how young he looked—about fifty-five. He was tall and reserved. But this man represented liberation. He was the one we were looking for.[11]

The American flag was raised that morning when MacArthur was in the camp, and the National Anthem was sung. Alice remembered, "There wasn't a dry eye in the place, believe me." In so many of the talks that Alice was to give, she tried to describe what it meant to see the Stars and Stripes again.

There was an unofficial flag ceremony as well. Two women had borrowed a flag from the rescuers and hung it over the principal doorway to the main building. Nurses had waved from the windows, and those standing on the roof of the portico over the door had raised their arms in jubilation. The crowd of internees below had spontaneously sung "God Bless America," and then followed with "Oh, say can you see . . ."

Alice was to say, "You never really know what something means until you lose it."[12]

Twenty-eight years later, Alice was to write the following:

As an Army nurse, following the fall of Corregidor, I was a POW of the Japanese in the Philippines for three years. During that entire period I neither saw our national flag nor heard our national anthem.

Under such conditions the flag becomes much more than stars and stripes on a piece of cloth, and the anthem, a great deal more than words set to music. They represent the difference between freedom and bondage.

Never will I forget the first time I saw our flag raised over the Internment Camp. It represented our precious freedom, but also the total commitment, even unto death, of our fighting men to liberate us. It would be impossible to express the depth of emotion one experiences at such a moment.

Those who would refuse to honor our flag and/or our anthem obviously have never been denied both.[13]

Later, Alice remembered, "You just didn't care who saw you cry; even the men were crying that day."

The raising of the American flag at Santo Tomas was a moment in which to think about all the anguish, to give meaning to all the loss. That afternoon, after MacArthur had left, the Japanese began to shell Santo Tomas. The west end of the main building where the women were housed was hit. There were ghastly things that, once seen, could not be forgotten, such as an old man searching amid the wreckage and dismembered bodies for his wife. Seventeen internees were killed in the shelling, and eighty were wounded.[14]

—◦◦◦—

Alice was soon back to work in one of the impromptu operating rooms, with young Terry Myers as an aide. Slowly, they were getting their strength back. They drank large quantities of coffee increasingly laced with powdered milk, as much as their shrunken stomachs could take. The liberating troops gave their own rations to the starving internees; after a few days had passed, food started to arrive. Arriving also were one hundred fresh army nurses.

Nine days after liberation, on February 12, sixty-six nurses—veterans of Bataan and Corregidor—left Santo Tomas to be flown to Leyte. In a sun-dazzled midmorning, as the nurses were loaded onto open trucks, Alice, Helen "Cassie" Cassiani, and Rita Palmer found Terry Myers and said good-bye.

The trucks drove as fast as possible through the burning city, past demolished buildings, the dead and the dying. There was artillery fire in the background. Nichols Field was too pocked with bomb craters for use; an army transport plane was waiting on Dewey Boulevard, which was being used as a runway.[15]

Alice's first flying experience proved to be a risky venture. In preparation for takeoff, the pilot ordered the nurses to crowd into the front of the cabin. As Helen Cassiani described, "We were literally piled one upon the other, four or five deep,"[16] with all praying that the plane's tail would rise from the pavement. They cleared the obstacles, banked over the smoking city, and headed for Leyte. Engine trouble forced them to land on American-held Mindoro off the southwest coast of Luzon. It was an unwanted delay, but there were doughnuts.

At one point, the nurses were deloused with DDT. The whole cabin of the plane was filled with a white mist, and the nurses joked that they could hear the bedbugs falling on the plane's floor. Considering the long-term effects, that incident may have been as dangerous as any portion of their extrication from Santo Tomas. The reality was that there were risks everywhere, as evidenced by the earlier engine trouble. It was decided that the nurses should continue to Leyte aboard two aircraft.

To the Allied world, the nurses were becoming a special cargo. They soon would be accompanied by news correspondents and photographers. Newspapers at home would carry front-page accounts of their progress back to the States, and all along the way there would be special attention and recognition.

In large part, all of this recognition stemmed from an appreciation for what these young women had done for "our boys." But there was also a morbid curiosity spawning horrible rumors of what the Japanese had done to the nurses. There was also the realization on the part of the American government and institutions such as the Red Cross that these nurses could be powerful instruments in building morale and support in that huge part of the war that was still to be fought. The nurses were flying out of the valley of the shadows of war and onto a spotlit stage.

They island-hopped toward Leyte in the lower Philippine archipelago. Leyte had been in the hands of the Allies since October 1944. It was home for the well-established 162nd General Hospital, which was chosen for the nurses as the place for a weeklong recuperation and debriefing. Seventeen of the nurses had to be hospitalized. Captain Maude Davison, who had done so much to keep the nurses together as a unit, was the sickest. She had an intensely painful intestinal blockage brought on by starvation. Nearly all of the nurses had problems that needed some attention. Alice was still recovering from dysentery. At first, there was a lot of sleeping on real beds; then, more and more activity, movies (Fred Astaire and Ginger Rogers), and ice cream.[17]

The press arrived as expected, and the army, both out of sympathy and because of its own desire for interviews and debriefings, moved the nurses to a more secluded convalescent hospital. Those nurses not hospitalized were housed in tents under tall palms, fronting a white-sand beach. Several of Alice's friends borrowed bathing suits, and then became aware of how thin and gaunt they really were.

The six nurses who had posed three years before for a photograph on a station platform in Cape Cod, stylishly dressed for travel and adventure, were photographed again on the beach in Leyte. They stand in baggy fatigues or wraparound hospital bathrobes, leaning into each other, holding hands. Alice wears her signature towel turban. They are all smiling, almost laughing. They are on their way home.

Class A uniforms were flown in from Australia. They weren't tailor-fit, but they set the nurses to primping. It is amazing how vain we all are, Alice thought, but she was as enthusiastic about dressing up as anyone. There was a reason to look their best. Near the end of their eight-week stay on Leyte, they were lined up in formation under the palms. There they were promoted to the rank of first lieutenant, and then General Guy Denit decorated each nurse with a Presidential Unit Citation and the Bronze Star.[18]

Later, Alice would say in an interview, "No one should be judged by his ribbons—everyone out there is fighting regardless of decorations." The credit, she said, went to the "boys who are coming back wounded, and those who will never come back."[19]

On February 20, the nurses began their long flight to California. At one point, the 1559th Army Air Force Base Unit provided the nurses with a "Bon Voyage Luncheon," complete with a printed menu. Alice filled open spaces on that menu with notes.

Alice discovered that she loved flying. The seats in the C-54Es in which the nurses flew were comfortable and conducive to sleeping, but Alice was too excited to sleep. She noted that they flew at seven thousand feet and at 190 miles per hour. The cover of the menu bore the symbol of the Air Transport Command and incorporated the flight route from Leyte to San Francisco. One could keep rough track of what was behind and what was to come. Captain Leora B. Stroup, Army Nurse Corps (ANC), was the chief flight nurse, and Alice noted her address. Alice thought it might come in handy if she required more information, as she intended to go back to the war. There was so much need, and she was considering becoming a flight nurse.

In 1,499 miles, they landed in Saipan and had their first hamburgers in three years. The Coke was served in large glasses that bore the phrase "Win for Liberty." Their next stop would be Kwajalein, where they would spend three hours before flying on to Johnson Island. At eight in the morning on February 21, they arrived at Hickam Field in Hawaii. The band played the National Anthem, and dinner was steak with all the fixings. They enjoyed their first hot baths in three years.

Next morning, there were opportunities to visit a hair salon and to go shopping. Alice had been waiting for the latter. The army had come across with $150 for each nurse (a very small fraction of what they were owed in back pay). Alice was feeling more like herself. All the ice cream was putting on some much-needed pounds. Alice told her chums that the two things she wanted most were to see her family and to find some nightlife. She went shopping for an evening dress.

The reporters and photographers followed the nurses. One of the latter got a good profile shot of Alice sniffing perfume. She was something of a connoisseur when it came to perfume. Back in Santo Tomas, she had filled several pages of her treasured notebook with the names of special and exotic fragrances in defense against the medieval smells of the camp.

In the photograph, cosmetics and other essentials just donated by resident nurses are crowded in a wondrous hoard on a table before her. The picture became quite popular, and was eventually published in many newspapers around the globe. Out on Okinawa, a lieutenant showed a newspaper copy to Alice's brother Ken.

Once again, Alice was taken with Hawaii. She wanted to buy a place on the islands someday and spend part of each year there. Two days after landing, the nurses got back aboard the C-54s for the last long hop to Hamilton Field in San Francisco. Hamilton's base command, guided and prodded by Washington, had been planning a welcome celebration for several weeks.

The nurses had been good copy even before their liberation. One patriotic poster featured a group of captured nurses dressed and capped in white, red lining showing from their turned-back blue capes, standing behind barbed wire and guarded over by a grotesque Japanese soldier with a rifle and long bayonet. The slogan reads "WORK! TO SET THEM FREE!"

Now the nurses had been rescued. On American ground, the planes taxied to form a surrounding backdrop, the doors opened, and the charming, feminine heroes came down the portable stairs. Historian Elizabeth Norman describes them as "recruiting icons, well-coiffed and smartly uniformed symbols of American womanhood serving their country and supporting the war."[20]

The nurses were ecstatic. In a moment, they would plant their feet on home soil. Captain Edith Shacklette, standing at the foot of the landing steps with her group close behind, had to hold back their enthusiasm. This homecoming in front of a large crowd of dignitaries, family members, and well-wishers ought to be done with a semblance of military order. Despite the intent, those nurses who had family waiting surged toward the crowd. When order was restored, the welcoming ceremony began.

Brigadier General Raymond Bliss, assistant surgeon general, gave the principal welcome.

"You," he told the nurses drawn up before him, ". . . will take your place with the pioneer women who have established the ideals on which we live." On the heels of this resounding affirmation of their service, the nurses were loaded into trucks and taken to their temporary quarters at Letterman Hospital.[21]

There were flowers on Ward A-2 at Letterman, with radios, boxes of Kleenex, and chocolates by their beds. The Quartermaster Corps had rounded up three hundred new uniforms in assorted sizes to assure better fit, and there were shoes and handbags as well. The Bataan Angels' new service to their country had begun. For a period of rehabilitation, those first few days back in the States were rather frenetic, despite the declaration that Sunday would be a day of rest.

Through the efforts of its district manager, the Pacific Telephone and Telegraph Company established a free long-distance connection for the nurses, who took turns calling home. Around two o'clock on Sunday afternoon in Brownville, the Zwickers got a call from their daughter. After more than three years, they heard her excited voice asking one question after another about the health and whereabouts of the family.

On Monday, the official welcome of the returning heroes was held on the hospital patio. The newsreel cameras rolled. General Hillman spoke, followed by Lieutenant Colonel Mary G. Phillips, assistant superintendent of the Army Nurse Corps. An ecumenical collection of clergy also spoke, followed by first lieutenants Rita Palmer and Rosemary Hogan, who had been wounded on Bataan and were awarded the Order of the Purple Heart. General Hillman handed to each nurse a personal letter of commendation and thanks from President Franklin Delano Roosevelt. The president had written: "You have served valiantly in foreign lands and suffered greatly. As your Commander in Chief, I take pride in your past accomplishments and express the thanks of a grateful nation."

The ceremony ended with short speeches from representatives of the American Red Cross, one of whom was Assistant Field Director Marie Adams, who had been a fellow internee at Santo Tomas.

Years later, Millie Dalton Manning, at nearly ninety-eight, remembered the homecoming in California: "All kinds of organizations and government agencies were giving us certificates and putting our names on buildings."[22] Though not quite what Alice had in mind when she had announced that she would search out "some nightlife," there was a whirl of social entertainment: On Tuesday, there was a dinner dance at the Officers' Club, and on Wednesday evening, a banquet at the Omar Khayyam restaurant. Later, Alice would tell a news correspondent, "People everywhere have been wonderful to me, and words are inadequate to express my appreciation for all that has been done for me since I started home."[23]

Slipped in between debriefings and social events was a trip to the shipyard at Richmond, California.

Alice had doubted whether people at home truly grasped the reality of the conflict or what was at stake, not having experienced true wartime hardship themselves. The women working at the shipyard helped to change her mind

Alice and her nurse comrades had much to process. For three years, it had seemed to them that they and all the troops in the Philippines had been sacrificed; for three years, they had waited for the rescue fleet to come over the horizon. Now they found themselves surrounded by laughing, well-fed, and fashionably dressed people. It was a startling shift in their circumstances, and it would take some time for them to adjust.

While all of the celebration upon their return may have aided the nurses in their rehabilitation, it did not eradicate what would now be called post-traumatic stress disorder. Alice would never have admitted to such problems, although she did say that one could not have experienced what they had without being changed. Still, she insisted, "The boys at the front are the ones who deserve the praise and thanks of the American people; we [the nurses] didn't really do anything."[24]

In general, and in public, the nurses made light of their inner problems, and claimed that their primary preoccupation was eating their way back to health. But dark memories and stress were there, and surfaced with renewed pain when wounded prisoners of war from Bilibid Prison Camp in the Philippines were brought to Letterman. The nurses knew these wounded men; twice they had been forced to leave them. Alice felt again the helplessness, the anguish, and the fury.

In Alice's scrapbook, there is a photograph of Alice and one of these wounded soldiers, taken outside the base hospital at Letterman. The three are holding between them a large placard honoring Alice and Millie Dalton, inscribed with a large eighth note and the name of the Western Defense Command Band. What the placard hides, but the captain's crutches disclose, is that the young officer standing with the two nurses has lost his left leg.

In Alice's mind, there was also a persistent sense of personal loss. Perhaps when the Japanese homeland was invaded, Lieutenant Fred Newell would be found alive, but she couldn't rid herself of the dreadful feeling that he was not coming back.

More and more, Alice became focused on getting back to Maine and her family. There were nieces and nephews she had never seen!

On March 1, 1945, she wired her folks in Brownville that she would be flying to Bangor, Maine, in two days. "Meet me there if possible," she added. On March 3, she sent another telegram: "Arrive Bangor 8:30 Sunday by air. Can hardly wait to see you all. Love, Alice."[25]

⏸ LIMELIGHT

The press camera caught Alice as she emerged from the plane's doorway. Somehow, the lens eliminated the effects of war and starvation; there was Alice, beautiful and projecting her good humor and her joy. She flew from LaGuardia on Northeast Airlines to Boston, and there the *Bangor Daily News*'s staff writer Nelle Penley was waiting, anxious to get the scoop.

Penley was an eleven-year veteran with the *News*, editor of the society page, and assigned reporter for Dow Air Force Base, but as they flew on to Bangor, she felt she was being interviewed by Alice. How were Drs. Knowlton, Robinson, and Ridlon and the "girls" from Eastern Maine General? Alice had no idea that Drs. Feeley and Savage were in the service, or that the hospital was participating in cadet nurse training.

When it came to information or opinions, Alice was not one who needed to be pumped—few of the Zwickers were. Alice had a mind for facts and dates, while feelings and opinions came hot off the grill, so to speak.

"The morale of the boys is high . . . if they can take it, so can I—that is why I feel so strongly about wanting to go back." She mentioned Luzon,

Leyte, and Iwo Jima. "Those wounded boys need nurses." The Japanese will never give up, she observed. She had heard the Japanese say that they could never go back home if they surrendered, and then she added that there are "quirks in the Japanese philosophy that the white man will never be able to understand."

Penley's pencil raced across the pad. How had Alice and the other nurses lived through prison camp?

The nurses had worked for as long as they had energy, and they had endured, Alice told the reporter. They used any excuse for a party, birthday or holiday. A long-hoarded can of Spam became Christmas turkey. "We knew that our day was coming and we could wait. . . . There were days when my spirits hit bottom, but those days were few and far between."

Alice told of hearing the guns to the north of the internment camp as liberation neared, and of seeing the bombers with their white stars, and then about the raising of the American flag at Santo Tomas. Then Alice turned to thinking about after the war. She would like to live in the tropics in the winter, or in California—except for Christmas, of course. She liked the Army Nurse Corps and was thinking she would make it her career.[1]

Alice nibbled the frosting on a chocolate cupcake. "It is hard to believe that I am almost home—I have dreamed about it so much. I can hardly believe that I am almost ready to see my mother."[2]

The plane banked and came in over the Penobscot and the white New England steeples of Maine's Queen City.

The Zwickers were waiting at the terminal: James and Mary; Catherine and her husband, John McDonald; Helena and her husband, Elton Tenney; and the youngest, Geraldine. Alice's two brothers weren't there, as Ken was on Iwo Jima, and Eli was attached to the 36th (Texas) Division on the Siegfried Line. The family group stood in their Sunday-best hats and coats, for it was still early spring, with an irrepressible joy springing upward like fountains from their seeming formality.

Nelle Penley described what happened next: "With a wild plunge, [Alice] landed in her mother's arms while her dad stood manfully by with an armload of flowers. But then she turned to her father and with a little girl's cry, pleaded 'Hold me tight.'"

A family supper was waiting at Helena and Elton Tenney's home on Coombs Street in Bangor. The party went on into the morning.

Alice was on a sixty-day rest leave, with thirty additional days optional. Despite this, the expectations and calls upon her to appear and to speak began within three days of her arrival home.

The first occasion was a joyous ordeal in the form of a homecoming celebration. The Brownville Grange Hall was patriotically festooned, and the head tables, arranged in the form of a V, were decorated with spring flowers and taper candles. Six hundred people arrived[3]—some from considerable distances, as evidenced by the cars parked in every nook and cranny up and down Church Street.

Young Earl Gerrish was nervous. He was one of ten Boy Scouts lined up to receive Alice at the Grange Hall door. What exactly were he and his fellow Scouts supposed to do or say? As far as he could see, there was a lot of needless hugging going on as Alice approached the Hall. But when Alice came through their lines, there were no problems at all. She stopped a moment to talk with each boy, and reminded Earl that she had been his babysitter years ago.

Isabel Lancaster was nineteen. She knew the Zwicker family well, having graduated from high school with Alice's brother Ken, but that evening in the crowd, she also felt nervous. When the time came for the receiving line, it seemed endless. Finally, she was standing in front of Brownville's hero. Isabel said something to the effect that she was representing her family. One of those intense smiles spread across Alice's face. She named Isabel's siblings and asked especially about her brother Reuben.

Properly welcomed, town manager Everett Gerrish escorted Alice to the head table, and the festivities began. The formal program had been planned by Mrs. Helen Stickney, matron of a musical dynasty in Brownville, who was, according to local tradition, one of the first women in the countryside to have voted in a presidential election. The town manager presented Alice with a shining identification bracelet and flowers.

Mary Zwicker got flowers as well. Hiram Gerrish, a lawyer from Milo, presented a photo of Alice arriving at LaGuardia Field on behalf of the postmaster of New York.

There had never been any intention of offering a short program. Choral singing was presented by two groups of girls from the grammar and high schools. And then, as a central piece, Nelson Brewer, whose voice was the pride of the village, sang. There were speakers, of course: lawyer Mathew Williams, who had been Alice's high school principal, and Myrtle Ladd, representing her father, the lumber baron of neighboring Barnard Township. Then R. D. Bickford, Alice's grammar school principal from the days when she wore those terrible, black-rimmed glasses, read an original poem written for the occasion.

Alice "graciously responded," adding that "she would do it [her Pacific duty] all over again . . . her only regret was the anxiety which she had caused her parents."

The evening was not over yet. A three-layer cake was presented to the head table. High school girls in white with Red Cross insignia helped to serve refreshments. The rich Scottish brogue of the Reverend Alexander Louden gave voice to prayer, and the night ended with a community sing. Thus began Alice's new tour of duty and her baptism into solo celebrity. Kindness and enthusiasm abounded. It was exhilarating and, for one still recovering her health, exhausting.

Duty called in earnest three days later. The venue was a Red Cross rally at Bangor's vintage City Hall. A clock tower added to the impressiveness of the building's redbrick exterior, while inside there was an auditorium which, by using both the floor and balcony, could seat two thousand. All of the big events in Bangor took place here, including boxing matches and performances by the Bangor Symphony Orchestra and the Trapp Family Singers. And now Alice would be standing at the podium with a thousand faces looking expectantly at her.

Across the city and in the surrounding communities, posters and flyers, which pictured Alice waving as she stepped from a plane, urged citizens to "be sure to hear Lieutenant Alice N. Zwicker." The "N" should have been "M" for "May," but who was counting errors? Alice was the only Maine woman ever to be held as a prisoner of war, and her presentation was going to be a major occasion! The city band would play, and leading local officials would speak in what was billed as an "unusually fine, patriotic program." Tickets were one dollar and would raise money for the Red Cross War Fund.

The morning of the Red Cross rally, Alice was interviewed on the Charlotte Carter Program, which was a regular feature on WABI radio. Newspaper announcements urged people to listen "to this thrilling program." A column in the same newspaper warned that tickets for the rally were going fast. The columnist adds, "Lt. Zwicker has a delightful personality and a keen sense of humor, and her talk will be interspersed with some of the humorous incidents which occurred during her thirty-nine months overseas with the ANC."[4]

That was the duty that fell on Alice: to be entertaining yet graphic enough at moments to make eyes moist. The appointed evening came, and Alice stepped forward, dressed in her neatly fitting uniform, bright with its ribbons and six service bars on the sleeve.

Behind her hung a large Red Cross banner, below which sat a crescent of important men, including President Arthur Hauck[5] of the University of Maine, the commanding officer and provost marshal at Dow Airfield, and the medical director at EMGH. Their presence was no comfort. As she began, she looked at Mary Zwicker's upturned face, beaming and truly happy. Alice guessed that there was tumult amid her father's hidden emotions.

The glowing account in the *Bangor Daily News* took up a full page. That same report may provide an answer to a puzzle: Why, in all of her public addresses, did Alice emphasize that the nurses had been well—even kindly—treated by their Japanese captors? The reporter for the *News* observed that Alice's remarks about the nurses' treatment "brought relief to people who have relatives in the Pacific theater who have been taken prisoner."[6]

That may well have been one purpose, but there seems to have been something deeper going on. Perhaps these statements were products of Alice's stubborn honesty. There were Japanese individuals, many of whom had been educated in America, who had endeavored to alleviate the suffering of prisoners on Corregidor and that of the internees at Santo Tomas. Still, it's easy to find Alice's insistence somewhat surprising, as she hated the brutality of the Japanese military machine and the men who had created and sustained it.

In another context, she noted that the Japanese cared no more for human life than the snap of a finger, and, when the atomic bomb was dropped over Hiroshima on Alice's birthday (August 6, 1945), she said that the government couldn't have given her a better present.[7]

Alice was not the only Angel of Bataan who insisted that the women had been treated by their captors with unexpected restraint and sometimes with kindness. There is another possible reason for their comments on how they had been treated. In November of 1945, Captain Rosemary Hogan wrote an article entitled, "What Did Not Happen to the Bataan Nurses." Soldiers in the U.S. Army and people at home could not believe that the nurses had escaped "beastly treatment." As has already been mentioned, ghastly rumors surrounded the returning nurses. It was told that Rosemary had been tortured and had lost both arms and her tongue.[8] Rumors of mutilation and rape threatened to rub out with ghoulish fabrications the truth about what these women had actually achieved and endured—the dirt, blood, bugs, starvation, and despair above which they rose, and through which they practiced good and faithful nursing. These women fought back to preserve the truth about their service. Of all the speculations concerning their reports on personal treatment, this one appears most likely.

That evening in Bangor, Alice endeavored to set the record straight and to balance the bad with the good. She told of sunsets on the China Sea, as well as eating scanty suppers of mush that tasted like chewing on old rags, and of those patients who had died of starvation and were piled at the end of a hospital corridor.

In his remarks following Alice's talk, Major Ballerino, provost marshal at Dow Air Force Base, focused on the climate in which the nurses had labored and suffered. He had been in the Philippine jungle, he said, and it was a "place of heat, rain, more heat and rain . . . a place of bugs and more bugs and snakes."[9] He made no mention of golden beaches or of waterfalls dropping into an emerald sea.

After her talk, a bouquet of American Beauty roses was presented to Alice, and the *Bangor Daily News* carried a picture of her handing Dr. Hauck a check for $800.18, the amount raised by the rally.

Alice's next speaking engagement was at the Piscataquis Country Club in Guilford, Maine, where the Kiwanis Club was holding its annual Ladies' Night—on the fourth anniversary of her enlistment, she noted. The event had been arranged by club president Mathew Williams, Alice's high school principal, and now, friend. There were some eighty people present, and the atmosphere was homey in comparison to the sea of faces she'd faced at Bangor.

According to the report in the *Piscataquis Observer*, Alice's talk sparkled with her personality and "ready wit." A natural talent was rising up in Alice's performances. As she once wrote to her sister Geraldine, "Zwicker women have never been known for brevity."[10] She might have added, nor for a shortage of forceful language when it comes to expressing their own opinions.

She described briefly her experiences in Bataan and Corregidor. The latter she described as "working with inadequate equipment, with a dwindling water supply, and amidst fumes of gunpowder and the consistent rumble and roar of gunfire."[11] The focus of her talk was life in Santo Tomas. During her description of what had transpired behind the camp walls, Alice denounced all those at home who griped against meatless Tuesdays and ration stamps. There was emotion and unmistakable sincerity when Alice ended with what the American flag meant to the starving internees when it was finally raised at Santo Tomas.

Again, there were red roses. The program ended with community singing and a dance.

Afterward, as a guest of the Williamses, Alice was glad for a chance to relax. The Williamses' daughter remembered that Alice sat down at the piano in their family living room and played "Red Sails in the Sunset."

During those first months at home, Alice lived in the limelight. Recognition came in unexpected ways. Ralph F. Bragg, who was brought

up in Milo, Maine, and had migrated to Boston, where he became a
well-known radio personality, wrote a song entitled, "MacArthur's Here
Again," which he dedicated to Lieutenant Alice Zwicker. The piece was
published as sheet music with a large likeness of the general on the front
page. There was also a photo of Bragg looking very distinguished in a
black bow tie, and another picture of Alice in her uniform. Years later,
when Alice's fame had languished, two of Alice's nieces sang that song
at a school assembly, and their aunt came to hear them.

But we are talking about the spring of 1945, when Alice was sought
across the state wherever there were war bond or Red Cross drives.
On April 6, 1945, she spoke before the combined houses of the Maine
State Legislature and attended a special reception held in the governor's residence at the Blaine House. Margaret Chase Smith, Maine's
worthy contribution to the U.S. Congress and the nation, was there. As
an added experience, Alice got to sleep the night before the reception
in the governor's mansion.[12]

Two weeks later, Alice was honored by Eastern Maine General Hospital with a banquet and the chance to speak to the hospital trustees,
twenty doctors, nursing staff, nursing students, and other associated personnel. As far as anyone could remember, it was the first occasion when
all those involved in the work of the institution had sat down together.
George Eaten, president of the hospital trustees, labeled the gathering
a "family party." The hospital was proud of the 121 staff members then
serving their country, and especially proud of Lieutenant Zwicker.[13]

It was all very pleasant. They ate amid red, white, and blue carnations
while a trio played soft music. The serious stuff would come later.

When Alice arose to speak, she spoke as a professional. This was a
different audience from what she had become used to, and she focused
her remarks on the situation she and members of the medical personnel
had faced in the Philippines: how that first Christmas of the war came
and went, with the medical staff so harried that no one knew what day
it was; of the forming of teams; and of the efficiency maintained despite
the deteriorating conditions. She had the audience's full attention as she
went on to describe hospitals on Bataan that were designed for hun-

dreds but served thousands. Her descriptions of the medical problems at Santo Tomas were graphic and specific.

Owen Brewster, Maine's senator—a man with a powerful forehead, serious brows, and stern eyes—followed Alice to the podium. He had flown in from Washington, DC, for this occasion, and he was not wasting his opportunity to speak on the momentous decisions that had to be faced. The experience of such fighting men and women as Lieutenant Zwicker spoke to the fact that people everywhere were entering a new world.

"We Americans," Senator Brewster said, "have been too concerned with building a continent" and not with "other countries and their conditions. . . . After all the suffering and sacrifices, we must be aware that the causes of new wars may be building even as present hostilities end."[14] It was a jarring way to end the reception party, but Brewster wanted to shake things up. There was still the invasion of the Japanese homeland to come, but even afterward, when the war was over, there would remain a real struggle to achieve peace in the world.

Alice understood. All the suffering and the human cost had not brought a new miraculous dispensation, but only a new chance for peace and justice. First things first; Alice knew that she must go back to the fight. She would endeavor to become a flight nurse, to help bring all those wounded boys home.

When her leave was up, the government offered a bonus of an additional twenty-two days of rest and relaxation at one of the several vacation facilities available to the military. Alice chose Santa Barbara. One could bring one's parents, and she was anxious to get hers into the sun and out of a Maine spring of slush and cold wind. But Irish and Jim feared they were too old for such a venture. Alice's mother was sixty-one, and her father sixty-nine.

Two years before, Mary had written to Alice: "I visited Dad a few days ago. [He was working at the shipyard at the time.] He is O.K. Not young anymore, as he and I both are far from young."

In another letter written a month later, Mary wrote: "We don't go anywhere. I am getting too old to go very much." Years of hard labor and going without for the sake of their family were catching up, and Alice was left with disappointment, her parents, with premature old age.[15]

Alice applied for nine weeks of flight nurse training, and while waiting for a spot was assigned to the 1380th Army Transport Command stationed at the air force base in Presque Isle, Maine.

Out in Okinawa, Alice's brother Ken got wind of Alice's determination to return to the Pacific. Portions of Ken's letters to Alice might be mistaken as love letters; they are love letters, in a sense. There was a deep bond between these two. Perhaps that bond was forged in the black, early morning hours of newspaper deliveries through the snowdrifts. Perhaps their close relationship was due to a twining of their genes or an effect of the poverty in which they grew up. Whatever the cause or causes, Alice and her brother Ken were close. They were knights-errant together, pitted against injustice.

Ken began a letter of remonstrance and advice to his sister, "Dearest Al."[16] There is loving concern in what follows, but nothing tender in the language:

> Damn it all, if you leave the States before I get there I'll kick your ——— [sic] all over town!! Now where in hell did you acquire the ——— idea that we couldn't win this ——— war without further assistance from *you*!?! Now by God you just stand at ease for a little while, will you?!! . . . So if you value my sentiments as much as you claim to, you'll just take that Presque Isle duty for a while. Write to me once or twice a week, send a quart [of whiskey] occasionally.[17]

The war would be over before Alice could earn her wings as a flight nurse.

(12)

NEW WINGS AND DELUGE

In March of 1945, the parents of Lieutenant Fred Newell received official word that he had been killed. He was posthumously awarded the Navy Cross for his participation in "operations of strategic importance in Manila Bay area involving hazardous missions such as reflect great credit upon the United States Naval Service." He had been taken prisoner on May 6, 1942. His end was tragic in a war of tragedies. He died when the unmarked "hell-ship" on which he and many other American POWs were being transported to the Japanese homeland for use as slave labor was sunk.[1]

Alice had known deep down that Fred would not be coming back; still, there was something of the forever lost in the news. She was glad that she was so focused and busy getting back into the war. In May 1945, just three days before V-E Day, she reported to the redistribution center at Santa Barbara for reassignment. There was a waiting list for getting into the Flight Nurse Training Program, so she was shipped back to Maine and posted at Loring Air Force Base in Presque Isle.[2]

There were always jokes about Loring, like, "What did you do to be sent to Siberia?" It was not Alice's first time there. During her tour of talks upon first arriving home from the Pacific, she spent two days in Presque Isle and on the "snowball base." Loring's public relations office saw to it that Alice was kept busy. She spoke before seven thousand people in various venues, including a public assembly at a high school. That number did not count those who listened to her broadcast message on WGAM. As an end to her visit, there was a dance held at the Officers' Club.

Everyone was eager to entertain this good-looking Angel of Bataan. Not only was she likable, but she was also a Maine girl who didn't mind the snow. The Arctic Search and Rescue Section got her out for a sled-dog ride behind two lines of Siberian huskies. It was a photo shoot across the open fields of Aroostook County farmland. She rode like a Russian countess, wrapped in a quilted robe and a hooded parka, with a fringe of fur surrounding her face.

One of the sled dogs at Loring was named Lena. She had been active in evacuating wounded from the snowbound battle lines of Belgium.[3] When Alice visited, Lena had just had a litter of seven pups. There was a mutual attraction between Alice and one of these baby huskies, so strong that it was decided to give the pup to Alice "as a token of . . . appreciation for the remarkable job she performed in speaking to the military and civilian personnel."[4]

When the pup later died of distemper, Alice experienced real grief. She found that the scars from what she had experienced overseas were very much present, exacerbated by the haunting feeling that what she loved would always be taken from her. But for Alice there was also that persistent joy in living. It resided deep inside her like a dance of the spirit that held hands with the will to "keep a-goin'."[5]

It was the greening of summer in northern Maine when Alice was posted to Loring as a nurse. The base was a busy place, serving as the headquarters for the North Atlantic Wing and concerned with flying Lend-Lease planes to England, along with personnel and equipment.[6] It was a life in motion, something Alice liked.

In July, she was sent as a medical attendant to Waltham, Massachusetts, and then flew back to Presque Isle. Apart from working at something she enjoyed, she was based only 160 miles or so from her parents in Brownville, and train service was good.

Alice had sent a quart of White Horse Whisky to Ken, who was still in the Pacific. The returning letter[7] began, "Darling, I love you!"—a sentiment that was seconded by two of Ken's buddies. The whisky, Ken said, had made Shenley's taste like raisin-jack. Ken also was enthusiastic about Alice's plans to buy a Buick convertible. When he was a kid working in Sam Cohen's clothing store in Brownville Junction, the chief perk had been driving the boss's Buick. But Ken was even more excited by Alice's news that she was thinking of writing a book.[8]

Then came the opening at the Flight Nurse School at Randolph Field in Texas. She kept in touch with her folks as she journeyed to Texas, and wired them on August 15, 1945, when she arrived at Randolph: "Wonderful place. Classes start tomorrow."

Alice was promoted to captain in August and graduated from flight nurse training on October 13.[9] With wings above her medal ribbons, she arrived at her next post, Mitchell Field in New York. Mitchell had been a major command and control base for both fighter and bomber groups, and remained a busy place. It was a good environment for Alice. As she said so often, she was "one of those screwballs who loved the service and was crazy about flying."

All of the Zwickers were back in Brownville for Christmas that year. Eli, the youngest in the family, had to sign up for additional time in the army in order to get leave. Like his brother and sister, Eli had seen tough service. He had been a medic in the rifle company, running and crawling from foxhole to foxhole along their section of the Siegfried Line. Mortar shells came in groups without warning. There was not all that much a medic could do—apply compress bandages, pour sulfonamide powder, and administer morphine—but it saved lives. After the war, fellow soldier Sam Prestman and his family invited Eli to visit them because Eli had saved Sam's life.

It was a white, joyous world there on Pleasant Street that Christmas. They all got together for a professional photograph, including the in-laws and two children of the next generation. In the photo, James Zwicker's quiet smile says it all: God's in His heaven, and we are all here.

Life was getting back to normal, but it was a very busy normal for Alice and her siblings.

Ken Zwicker got married in January 1946. His bride, Marilyn Coy, had grown up in the neighboring town of Milo. She and Ken had been a couple before the war. She had since been to college and was trained as a nutritionist. Marilyn smilingly remembers that the winter cold drove them to elope. They rode south all night on the train toward New York City for a splurge before settling down to get Ken through four years of college. They stayed at the Algonquin in the middle of the lights. Alice joined them, bringing two large stuffed animals—a bear for herself and a floppy-eared lamb for Marilyn. During a bash in the Latin Quarter, they had three bottles of champagne at thirty dollars a bottle.

The survivors among the defenders of Bataan and Corregidor had formed an organization "dedicated to those persons living or dead who fought against overwhelming odds against the enemy at the outbreak of World War II." They held their first convention in April at the Hotel Bradford in Boston. Alice joined enthusiastically, serving jointly with Helen Cassiani as corresponding secretary.

At Union Station in Bangor, Maine, Mary Zwicker greeted the young, dark-eyed, vivacious Terry Myers as she stepped down from a railroad coach. Almost reverently, Terry was following in Alice's footsteps.

It was Terry's first trip to the Atlantic coast. She had been lost for an hour and a half in New York, but she liked the big city, and Boston, too. Earlier, she had visited Alice at Randolph Field and was full of the excitement about beginning her training as a nurse at Eastern Maine General Hospital, Alice's alma mater. For the next few years, Terry would become a sometimes tumultuous adjunct to the Zwicker family. In a letter to Alice, her father wrote that Terry was "getting along O.K.," and then added that at that moment, Terry "had the radio going full blast in the dining room."

A new, or renewed, interest had taken over Alice's life. She was involved with Robert "Bob" Blezard Dameron, the Texan she had met as an internee at Santo Tomas.

Dameron had been a district manager for the Southern California Fruit Exchange (Sunkist) when he was interned by the Japanese. He was nine years older than Alice, but that hardly mattered; a close friendship had become more than that.

Alice visited him in California, and by the time she returned to Mitchell Field, she had decided to marry Bob. It was a big decision, driven in
part by a deeply felt need to settle down and have a family. Alice was
thirty; it was time. Once the decision was made, it had all her heart behind it; that was her way. Her unfaltering loyalty sprang from the same
openhearted source. As one of her close friends observed, "Alice was
loyal to a fault." She made Bob her first beneficiary of military benefits.[10]

On October 7, 1946, Captain Alice was posted as chief nurse at
Morrison Air Force Base in West Palm Beach, Florida. Morrison was
another of those important airfields winding down after the full-out
effort of the war. The base had served as the air transport and training
headquarters for the Caribbean Wing of the Air Transport Command.

With winter in the offing, it was a great place to be, but Alice planned
a Christmas Eve wedding; after that, she would leave the service and
follow Bob to Kansas.

Nelle Penley, the *Bangor Daily News* social correspondent who had
covered Alice's triumphant return to Maine after the war, wrote the
wedding account for the Bangor paper:

PRISON CAMP ROMANCE BLOSSOMS

A romance which had its beginning in Santo Tomas Jap prison camp was
culminated in marriage on Christmas Eve at 8 o'clock . . . when Captain
Alice May Zwicker became the bride of Robert B. Dameron of Kansas
City, Mo. . . . The chapel at Morrison Field was beautifully decorated with
poinsettias and greens . . . Chaplain Uriel K. Perrigo officiated, reading
the double ring service in the presence of a large gathering of friends.

First Lieut. Cherry E. Parnell, ANC, was maid of honor, and the best
man was Captain Robert P. O'Shaughnessey, AMC. The bride, who was
given away in marriage by Captain J. McInerney, Adjutant at Morrison
Field, wore a beige dress uniform which she complemented with a cor-
sage of gardenias.[11]

A reception was held in the decorated nurses' quarters, replete with
a Christmas tree. The honeymoon was spent in Florida, after which
Dameron returned to his work, which had taken him to Kansas. Alice
would go to Maine for a brief visit after she had completed her separa-

tion from the service, before she went west to make a new home for her husband at Clyde Manor, Kansas City. They hoped to be able to return, at least occasionally, to the islands of the Pacific, where many of their friends lived.

Those were the happy plans.

The physical examinations were one of those hoops one had to jump through when leaving the service prefunctory.

"What a blow!!" Alice said later. After her examination, she was admitted to Pratt General Hospital at Coral Gables with a diagnosis of "minimal pulmonary tuberculosis." The aftereffect of those night shifts on the contagion ward at Santo Tomas was touching her like the reach of a skeletal hand.

Mary Zwicker had told Alice's father that there was bad news in the offing; she had seen a warning in her tea leaves. On January 14, 1947, James wrote to his daughter:

> You don't know how I felt this afternoon when I came home and heard that you wanted to speak to me. . . . What does your husband think about you and he being separated for six or eight months. How far will you be from where he is? . . . Mother said you felt bad because you were married, but don't do that because it wasn't any fault of yours. I hope time doesn't go too slow and that you'll be O.K. in a few months.

Her father admonishes her to "keep praying and her chin up." He ends the letter with, "From your loving old Dad."[12]

Another letter came from Ken, who was by then studying at the University of Maine:

> Dear Swish:
>
>   I don't need to tell you how damned sorry I am that your luck has taken another dive to the bottom. . . . [We can talk] about everything being for the best, [but] the ugly fact still remains that it takes plenty of old-fashioned guts to face such a situation. . . . It's easy as hell to give pep talks—the old "cheer up" routine . . . that's why I'm not gonna give you one. I don't think you need it anyway. If I know "the Captain," you'll make out. . . . Maybe the chow will be good or something—or maybe you'll

make a fortune playing blackjack! Any way you look at it, it ain't good, but if I know you, you'll find *something* to put on the credit side of the deal.[13]

As a good brother, Ken shifts and fills the next pages with humor. He reaches back to the characters and situations they had known in Brownville by making analogies to his own present existence as a student.

Terry wrote as well. She had thought that Alice "looked like hell" the last time she had seen her. It was a letter that might have been written by a daughter to her mother. She wished that she might take this illness on herself. She ended with news from Maine, noting that she'd gone sledding with Alice's father.

In 1947, streptomycin was undergoing extensive experimental testing for use in fighting tuberculosis, but drug therapy for the dreaded disease was still in the future. Alice knew the drill awaiting her all too well. Standard treatment called for bed rest, regimented diet, fresh air, and months of little or guarded activity. Alice vowed to follow the rules and get better.

She was also determined to be as close to her new husband as possible. In less than a month, she was transferred to Fitzsimons General Hospital, a huge army institution whose new main building was the largest structure not only in Aurora, Colorado, but in the whole state. Inside the lobby and up the staircase, one had the feeling of being in an Art Deco temple to modern medicine; nonetheless, day after day spent in Ward F-2 was a tough world, and monotonously the same.

Alice's husband came for several days, dropping in from his continual travels. Her sister Catherine, along with her husband and daughter, Alice Mary, came at the end of May. Alice wrote, "So *good* to see them all!" Her brother Eli also arrived for a week with two of his chums, Len Swazey and "Popeye" Marsh. Fitzsimons's composure survived. That visit was followed by Bob Dameron (the "Darling") returning for two weeks. Alice wrote how wonderful his visit was. "He was so good to me!"[14]

Alice moved again to be closer to Bob; she left Fitzsimons at the end of August and went to the Veterans Hospital in San Fernando, California.

Her treatment was more rest. The day following her arrival in California, she retired as a captain in the Army Nurse Corps. Then, four days after Christmas 1947, the truly dark days began. Bob told her that he was afraid of TB. He wanted a divorce. He told her on his birthday; "What a horrible day!" Alice wrote. There would be months of misery to follow, even while her health was improving.

Over a year in the hospital crept by before Alice was considered well enough to come home for several months of additional convalescence. The newspaper assumed that she would be returning to California to be with her husband.[15] Knowing Alice's loyalty, perhaps she still hoped that this might be the case.

Convalescence was a relative term in Alice's vocabulary. Soon after she arrived home, she was invited to a meeting of the Milo Nurses Guild and asked to talk about her war experiences. Alice had worked with most of the guild's members following her graduation from training. She also traveled to New York for several weeks to visit a nurse and a friend who was being sent to Germany for two years.

The big event of the summer was the Zwicker family reunion held in August, in conjunction with Brownville's Old Home Weekend, which the newspaper reported was an "event not to be forgotten." There was a feast at the table in the Zwicker parents' new home on Windy Hill. After the meal, they gathered for "one of their always much enjoyed hymn sings. It was a grand time."[16]

Whatever Alice's schedule, it seems to have been beneficial. Near the end of her stay at home, she wrote: "Six months home—health excellent—weight fat—marital status, nearly free. Feel fine mentally and physically. No lie! Time is the healer of all things!"[17]

13

THROUGH THE VALLEY
OF THE SHADOW

A nticipation had mixed with anxiety among the Angels of Bataan as they returned from the war. Would the homes they were so anxious to reach be changed? Had the world they so often revisited in the huddled warmth of their memories wasted away? And concerning that huddled warmth inside, what about the Angels themselves? Had the experience of war touched everything that had been sure and comfortable? War seemed to change everything deep down, where it matters most.

When Alice arrived back in the States, she had thrown herself into being her normal self. Even before her return, she had been looking for a lovely, long dress in which she would dance the night away. When the war ended, she married, trusting that she had found a lifetime mate with whom she had shared so much, and with whom she could start a family.

Now the good news was that she apparently had overcome the tuberculosis and could explore her intention of spending her summers in Maine and her winters in California. She would go to college, and she would follow Ken's encouragement and write. She would raise some hell, probably, but her real intention was to search until she captured a new and larger significance in her life.

Alice spent the winter of 1948–1949 in California, with the exception of a trip back to Maine for Christmas. In March, she typed a fifteen-page letter, single-spaced, to her brother Ken.[1] As she explained, it was an exercise in writing, and perhaps would be incorporated in the beginning of a book she would like to write. Her thoughts were running faster than her fingers, for there was so much that had been going on. Alice writes, "to hell with the punctuation," and with that begins to tell Ken a saga that for several months has dominated her life.

She was not proud of some of the things that had happened, for there was much in this winter interlude that was silly—even ugly. If one were honest, there was much in this account that arose from her conditioning experience as a prisoner in the tunnels of Corregidor and in the captive world of Santo Tomas. She had been grasping for something hopeful—miraculous, maybe—and reaching out for protective alliances, while, at the same time, going with the flow and determined to keep the peace, even if it meant being subservient.

As Alice's report to her brother begins, she is living in a small apartment in San Diego with a close friend whose first name is Ruth.[2] Both are going to college.[3] A third member of their small circle is Alice's boyfriend, Don Kempton, a fellow student and former fighter pilot. They are a close group.

Bataan nurse Eleanor Garen once noted that war had taught her comradeship, and now that the war was over she was afraid to be alone. There was something akin to this in the togetherness of this trio, something of the tightness between special friends that had been so important to Alice for survival at Santo Tomas. Alice and Ruth would often stay up into the early morning hours, drinking coffee and discussing what had gone on during the day.

There is a fourth person who shares this inner circle for a time. Alice uses only her first name, Venus. She is Alice and Ruth's landlady, an older woman who lives in a nearby apartment. As Alice's narrative continues, Venus emerges as a dark person with a cloak of domination about her shoulders, who, by the end of Alice's account, attempts to turn friends against each other.

In the beginning, however, she appears to be deeply concerned and even motherly, visiting the "girls" frequently and talking at length—lecturing, actually—on the "I Am Activity," a religious group of which she is an avid disciple.[4]

For a time, Alice and Ruth find the concepts of "I Am" interesting, albeit complicated. They try to understand as much as they can. Shortly after Alice returns from Christmas in Maine, she becomes uneasy about Venus's motherliness. Alice writes that, "She seemed to have a fatal fascination for [me]." Moreover, it soon becomes obvious that Venus considers herself an expert on everything, including being a critic of Ruth's coffee. Ruth, being Swedish (and a connoisseur of fine coffee), is "damned mad about that."

Alice and Ruth return to their classes, and still Venus comes over whenever she pleases, staying late. With this distraction, Alice finds herself having to study until four in the morning for exams. Her grades remain high, but Alice describes the strain as "unbelievable." There is no privacy, especially when Don is there. Alice becomes determined to keep the peace; it seems the most important thing to do under the circumstances. In her account to Ken, she writes that he would have been surprised to see how hard she tried, but nonetheless, the crack between herself and Venus widened.

That crack widens to a gap when Alice catches a cold and Venus becomes annoyingly concerned. One day Alice returns late from classes, having done some shopping; Venus meets her at the door and orders her to get out of her clothes and into bed. Alice is furious. As she tells Ruth, not even her own mother would have done that. She would have known better.

The narrative in Alice's letter to Ken shifts momentarily from Venus to Bob Dameron, her ex-husband.

Bob had not wanted Alice to know where he was, nor was she interested in knowing, but through a coincidence she had been in contact with him. By accident, the bank in which both had accounts sent her Bob's bank statement and canceled checks. Alice admits that she felt a certain satisfaction in finding out where he was when he had not wanted her to know.

Alice forwarded the bank statements to Dameron, and he returned the favor by sending Alice hers, which, in the mix-up, he also had received from the bank. There was a brief note, saying that he hoped she was feeling well. The more she thought about that note, the more she wanted to write him a letter. The love she had felt for him was gone, but so was the hate.[5]

Alice notes to her brother that hatred warps one's whole outlook, and is something you should rid yourself of, as soon as possible.

Finally, she wrote a letter to Bob that required no response; after all, they "had been such good friends for such a long time." Weeks later, there was an answer:

> Dear Swish:
>   Don't fall over! After all, I think we both admit that two people never meant to be *better friends*. Right? Was glad to receive your letter and to learn that you are now *all O.K.* and feeling fine. It makes me feel better to know that, and am glad that you are doing well in your studies in school.[6]

At this point Venus reenters Alice's written account. She is now hovering, scheming, and trying to get Alice and Dameron back together. The situation was troubling enough, but it was to become even more complicated and disruptive. In the course of all her meddling, Venus introduces Alice and Ruth to Cecil Stokes and his cause.

Cecil Stokes was a well-educated visionary on the verge of introducing a new treatment for the mentally disturbed. He had named the treatment and process "Auroratone." Both Cecil's wife and daughter were very involved in the project, just as Alice, Ruth, and Don Kempton would soon become. Cecil's enthusiasm had hypnotic qualities. Alice wrote that it was as though they previously had met somewhere and had been separated for a long time.

Cecil had been a newspaperman in Florida and was returning from a trip to the West Indies on board a boat when the conception of the Auroratone experience revealed itself. There was a sunset reflected on

a slight ocean swell. A waltz was being played on the deck above, and
the music, the colors of the sunset, and the motion of the swell together
became one engulfing, calming beauty. Cecil's Auroratone would com-
bine, on film, changing abstract color patterns with appropriate music.
What healing might be accomplished in psychiatric and veterans' hospitals across the country with Auroratone![7]

Stokes's creations utilized forming crystals filmed with time-lapsed
photography under polarized light, synchronized with quiet, soothing
airs from such musical scores as "Claire de Lune," Stephen Foster's
"I Dream of Jeannie," or Schubert's "Ave Maria." Special also was his
choice of Bing Crosby as soloist in several Auroratone productions.[8] It
does not appear that Alice ever met Crosby, but in her scrapbook there
are several large Auroratone promotion photos of him, and she wrote to
her brother Ken that she felt she knew him.

Cecil was soon a regular visitor to Alice and Ruth's apartment, where
he found a ready and admiring audience for his spirited descriptions
of his films and the Auroratone Foundation. Alice became convinced
that he was a caring and creative human being, a "regular guy," as she
phrased it to her brother. She introduced Cecil to her boyfriend, Don
Kempton, and soon "the trio" had invested five hundred dollars each
in Stokes's project. Cecil gave them each a small parcel of land in the
desert where his foundation's new headquarters would be built and
promised them all positions on his staff, which at that point consisted
only of Cecil's wife and daughter.

Both Ruth and Alice had grown disillusioned with college classes,
and with all that was now unfolding with Stokes, they left school. Ken
Zwicker, despite his high estimation of education, agreed that it was
probably a good move. He wrote:

> As far as school is concerned, you have proved to yourself and any other
> persons who are interested that you are capable of handling it without any
> trouble! Your ranks were *damned* good, from any standard, and especially
> good when one considers the fact you have been away from anything that
> resembles a college classroom for YEARS!!

But there are many valid reasons why you shouldn't stay with it! The first, of course, is the fact that you don't *like* it! And although there need be no others, an outstanding one, as it seems to me, is the basic fact that you are expending good energy in the wrong direction! . . . You have a hell of a supply of energy to get out of your system—not necessarily all physical, either, of course. With a temperament like yours, the *extremely* unusual life you have had, and the entire collection of feelings, emotion— call it what you will—I can see no better method or channel through which to direct it, than *writing!*[9]

Ken's view seemed a reasoned response compared to the mayhem in which Alice would soon find herself. It seemed that at one time, Cecil had also been involved in the "I Am Activity," and there was already conflict between him and Venus. Now Venus was growing desperate, as she felt herself excluded from the trio's preoccupation with Cecil and his project. She announced that she should be in charge of any money being invested in the Auroratone Foundation.

Cecil's emotional dam burst. The trio got Venus and Cecil separated. It was decided to get him out into the country, where he could calm down. On the way, Cecil decided that he wanted to hear "Far Away Places," which Crosby was recording for Auroratone. The only place where a piano could be found was a bar. Alice took over the piano, others in the bar joined them, time passed, and according to Alice, they all got "a little high," except for Cecil, who became decidedly drunk. That evening, Alice must have sung "Far Away Places" at least a hundred times in an attempt to calm the distraught inventor of Auroratone.

Venus was sure that Alice and Ruth were getting Stokes drunk for their own nefarious purposes. Then, as tension grew in every corner, Venus made the mistake of calling Alice a liar, and the two had it out on the stairs to Venus's apartment.

At one point Venus cautioned, "Alice, I have a powerful will." And Alice exploded: "Venus, don't try to frighten me, because until you've seen me in action, you don't know what a powerful will is. I'll fight with any weapons, fair means or foul, so don't push me anymore."

Venus didn't.

Alice was recovering her Zwicker self. She moved out of the apartment and stayed with friends, while Ruth went to look for another apartment. By then, spring had come, and Alice was thinking of Maine. She hoped to be home for Ken's college graduation.

That summer, Cecil sent her his picture with the inscription, "Love and Stuff from one old stinker to another—always and all ways! Cecil." As spring blossomed, Bob Dameron, the manipulating Venus, and Cecil Stokes with his Auroratone project, became incidents in the past—islands left behind in the river of Alice's travels in search of an ocean that could provide a reservoir of significance and peace.

Ken Zwicker, in his answer to Alice's long saga, thanked her for sending him a subscription to *Time* magazine, which he had wanted for some time, and for the copy of Joshua Liebman's bestseller, *Peace of Mind*.[10]

Alice was enthusiastic about the book and had found it hugely useful. It had a message for her world, struggling out of the experience of the war. If one wished "to contribute to a healthy society . . . [one] must have peace of mind first." Modern psychology "must be supported by religion—an accumulation of spiritual wisdom, at-homeness in the universe." Liebman proposed that with the advent of psychology, "religion was becoming mature." Together with religion's understanding of that which is within and yet greater than ourselves, psychology's knowledge was "floating man off the submerged ledge of grief and perplexity."[11] "We feel our aloneness and are frightened by our fragility. . . . [W]hen we grow afraid of life and desire, let us have the sense of the trustworthiness of the universe, of its encompassing embrace and its sustaining care, and let us know that we can never travel beyond the arms of the Divine." There seemed to be so much sense in Liebman's writing—so much Alice felt she needed to hear.

Before Alice left for a summer in Maine, she attended the second annual convention for ex–prisoners of war.[12] The Hollywood Roosevelt Hotel was crowded. It was good to be with those who had shared what she had suffered through; there was no need to pretend or try to explain. When Alice met Sergeant Harry Morris in the lobby, they studied each other for a moment, then Alice rushed over to him, stood on her tiptoes, and kissed him on the cheek. The last time she had seen that face, she had been working to save his left eye and wiping blood from around his shell wound.

As the convention drew to a close, veteran Orman Jacques rose and proposed that Captain Alice May Zwicker be elected Miss Bataan for the 1950 National Convention. The newspaper headline read "COR-REGIDOR NURSE NAMED MISS BATAAN." Alice replaced starlet Nan Leslie, who had previously held the honor.

In June, Alice attended Ken's graduation from the University of Maine. Their father, mother, sister Catherine, and her daughter, Alice Mary, along with brother Eli, were there. Ken had done his college work in three and a half years, but it had been a long three and a half years, as his wife knew well. They had so little money. Once, when commuting to school from Brownville, Ken had to patch his tires five times.

The spring and summer of 1949 in Brownville were noted for two things: a forest fire that burned buildings and a large acreage to the north, and erratic weather. Alice did not get home in time to see the night sky reddened by the fire, but she did experience the up-and-down weather. On one day, it was so hot that the Lewis Mill did not open, while others were so chilly that the dandelions didn't open. Nights were chilly as well.

In July, Alice was glad to get away for a visit to New York City. She left that city a member of the "Pipe Society," at an establishment called the English Chop House. Years later, she would go back to the old tavern, where the proprietors kept her long-stemmed "churchwarden" pipe waiting. She would be living in Brooklyn, New York, then and would take her young niece, Lynn Zwicker, to the Chop House as part of a high school graduation gift and an introduction to the world outside Brownville.

Early in her summer stay in Maine, Alice caught a cold that hung on and developed complications. She was not really over it when, in the fall, she headed back to California. Terry Myers and her husband, Al Johnson, were driving to Al's home in North Dakota, and Alice rode with them. She went by bus from there to California. The following letter[13] to Ken Day of the American Ex-Prisoners of War Association best tells what transpired next:

Dear Ken,

The photo received, and thanks very much. Was glad to receive your brief note and decided I'd answer same. I left California in May and came to Maine for the summer, per schedule. Got a bad cold soon after my arrival here, which developed into a virus infection. Result? Saw my doctor in San Diego in September for my routine check-up, and now I'm chasing the cure again!

Yep, the ole TB bug has caught up with me again. I didn't have to go into the hospital; I'm doing sack time at home. Six months, the doctor said, and I started Oct. 1st. Only hope it's no longer. If it is, I'll have to go back to the sanitarium, and they'll start pneumothorax on that side.[14] So I'm keeping my fingers crossed on that convention deal. D— it all, why do these things always have to happen? I've really been planning on the convention, but I can't hardly compete with the Tubercle Bacillus, now can I??? But we shall see. I certainly do enjoy that paper XPW Bulletin, no lie, really filled with scoop.

Ken, I'm not permitted to do much, but if there's anything at all that you think I have brains enough to understand, I'd be only too glad to do it, believe me. Please don't hesitate to ask me. Guess they should have chosen a healthier "Miss Bataan."

Sincerely,

Alice

Alice had been back in Brownville since the second week in October. The crossing of fingers didn't help. In July, Alice was admitted to the Bangor Sanatorium. There was fresh air, sunshine, and good care, but life was on hold day after day for seven months. What was worse, that hold was not secure. There was faithful family, including her brother Ken, who was city editor for the *Bangor Weekly* and *Sunday Commercial*. Alice's nephew Rod Tenney remembers going to the sanatorium to visit his aunt; he had to wait in the corridor while his parents visited her, because children were not allowed further entry.

What followed were four years of ups and downs and of stays in several institutions. Alice began to look for vocational training—something positive that someone with limited strength could accomplish. In 1952, she found a possibility through patient training in radio programming.

She was soon planning and directing a two-and-a-half-hour popular musical program called *Variety Carnival*. The only worry on the part of those in charge of the program was that Alice would work too hard. The chief of special service wrote:

> The patient has displayed an exceptionally wide knowledge of popular music. . . . Her radio presentation has been warm, friendly, and natural, conveying to her audience the feeling that she, too, is enjoying the recordings. . . . She has accomplished an unusual amount of work to date . . . and has displayed a high degree of initiative and stick-to-it-iveness. . . . She is an extremely pleasant person to work with, and we would give her a rating of "excellent" in cooperation and dependability.[15]

The music program was great, but she was traveling in a gray valley with the knowledge that the tubercle bacillus was still there in one of her lungs. Moreover, Alice was all too aware that her country was at war again, in Korea. She could picture with anguish what was going on. All she could do—she, who was trained for air evacuation—was send care packages to soldiers.

In response to one such package containing a cake, she received a letter of thanks from the chaplain of the 31st Infantry Regiment, a regiment with which Alice had been associated on Bataan. On a day close to Christmas, the chaplain of the 31st and his houseboy had taken the package by jeep to an outpost. Attached to the letter was a hand-printed note from Private First Class Wallace E. Dove. It was also signed by six other men of Charlie Company. Two mortar rounds had come in, but then it was quiet and the chaplain produced the box. "I could hardly believe it," wrote Wallace Dove, "when the Chaplain gave me the wonderful package."[16]

Although the radio work and the letter from the guys in Korea was something to grab hold of, the tuberculosis was becoming worse. The doctors began to talk of a pneumonectomy. Alice knew that meant the removal of a lung by a radical operation known for its risk and long, painful recovery. The shadows in the gray valley became darker, and within them was the beginning of despair.

Because Rutland, Massachusetts, had considerable elevation and "good air," it became the home of a well-known sanatorium. There was a veterans' hospital there as well, and both institutions had the benefit of medical support from facilities in Worcester, located only some twelve miles away. The Veterans' Hospital at Rutland was a good choice for Alice.

The Roman Catholic chaplain became one of Alice's regular bed-side visitors. For some reason, he seemed the only chaplain around. Perhaps Alice told him about the young priest at the hospital in Santo Tomas, who had vowed he would pray her into the church. Whether or not she did, Alice's search for strength and meaning was moving in that direction.

Perhaps it was this chaplain at Rutland who introduced Alice to one of the most important figures in her life, the Reverend George J. McKeon, who became known as "Father Mac."[17] Before she met him, Alice had decided that men could be placed in three categories: questionable, im-mature, and worse than that. Years later, she would write to her niece: "Thank God for my gift of faith and my Father Mac—I could never have made it without both."[18]

Father Mac was two years older than Alice. He had begun his study at Holy Cross, entered the Society of Jesus in 1941, completed his the-ology studies in 1951, and earned a master's degree in psychology from Weston College. In 1954, Father Mac was back at Holy Cross, where he established the Counseling Center and began the formation of a depart-ment in experimental psychology. He was an unusual young man.

One of his fellow priests and teachers described his ability and char-acter as the joining of "Ignatian levelheadedness and ability to go to the heart of things [with] a Franciscan enjoyment and love of life in its smallest aspects."[19] In his study and work for a PhD at Fordham University, Father Mac had done special work with patients and staff at one of the larger TB hospitals in New York City. His experience and background soon made him a lecturer and a traveling consultant on high standards of patient care.[20]

This was the man who was to become Alice's close and special friend. He guided Alice's conversion to the Roman Catholic faith, and she turned to him in the darkness and pain that were to come with the re-moval of a lung.

14

AND YET THE DANCE

In January 1954, when Alice was back in Brownville convalescing with her folks on Windy Hill, she wrote a get-well note to family friend James Mealey, who had also had serious surgery:

> It seemed useless to write sooner because one hardly feels like going over mail. On 7 January, approximately 10 months ago, I had my first stage of chest surgery, followed by the second stage on 2 February. While our diagnoses were not the same, nevertheless it's a pretty painful business. At least I found it so. I do sincerely hope that you are improving daily. . . . Remember you are in our prayers.[1]

A month later, Alice was visiting her friend and protégée, Terry Myers Johnson, at Bergstrom Air Force Base in Texas, when her mother wrote that Mealey had suffered a heart attack. Alice wrote a longer letter to the man who had been so helpful to the Zwicker family:

> I have thought of you so many times in the past months. I wonder if you realize that in our part of the country you are a legend, Mr. Mealey. Do you know that I personally can't remember any other state policeman. I may be of small consolation to you, but believe me, you have many praying for your

recovery. . . . There is very little one can say, because it's always so easy to be an armchair philosopher. But one thing I do believe with all my heart, and that is that God sends the greatest crosses to those He loves most. It is often very hard to believe that when we are those with the crosses. But I've found that no matter how bad things gets, it could *always* be worse, and I remember at such times that the greatest cross God ever sent was to the one person he loved most in the whole world—His Only Begotten Son. . . . And be assured of a continued remembrance in my poor humble prayers. Say one for me, will you?[2]

Perhaps there is something of Father Mac's theology in this letter; certainly Alice's newfound Catholic faith is speaking, along with her acquaintance with pain. Alice was struggling up and out of a harrowing experience. Her brother Eli remembered that her radical surgery had left an incision scar down her chest, which followed the curve of her rib cage to her back and upward to her shoulder blade. There had been over ninety stitches. With the postoperative trauma and pain came dreams and hallucinations. She awoke one night to see a Japanese officer in full uniform and sword staring at her from the foot of her bed, and there was the repeated appearance of a human heart, alone and beating in an upper corner of the room.

Twenty years later, Alice wrote to her niece Jayne, whom, with the Zwicker penchant for nicknames, she called "Bugsley," or simply "Bug":

Because I am and have ever been "Aunt Alice," you cannot *know* the anguish, grief, and heartache—at one period on the verge of suicide—that I have endured. . . . Yet, in retrospect, Bug, I wouldn't change any of it.

Slowly, her remaining lung partially compensated for the loss of its twin. She would never again have her original quickness or stamina, but Alice was regaining her health.

One indicator of her recovery was the forceful letter she wrote to President Dwight Eisenhower in April of 1955. That epistle was filled with her shock and indignation that the conviction of John Provoo, for treason and collaboration with the enemy, had been overturned.[3] The case was well known to veterans of Bataan, and there had just been an article in *Cosmopolitan* magazine that reviewed the allegations of Sergeant Provoo's admiration for the Japanese and his cooperation with the enemy during the battle of the Philippines.[4]

There was no doubt in Alice's mind that Provoo was guilty. She didn't blame the president for Provoo's release, but someone had botched the legal process. In her words, "The Rosenbergs, Dickenson, Batchelder, and Schwable were babes in the wood compared to this guy, and he is free!" Alice was furious. The Alice of earlier years was bouncing back.

There were setbacks. Her father died that May. She looked at a photo of herself as a young child, riding high on her father's shoulders, and wept.

His passing came just a few days after she had registered at the Sadie Brown Collegiate Institute in New York City. The school was approved by the Regents of the University of the State of New York and had a recognized executive secretarial course, which she had decided to take, with Father Mac's urging and, as Alice felt, God's leading. Three years later, in 1958, she got her diploma.

In September of the same year that her father died, Alice went on a weeklong retreat at Lady Isle, Portsmouth, New Hampshire. Each day started at 6:00 a.m. with prayer, followed by Mass and Communion; it ended at 9:00 p.m. with the Rosary and conferencing, but in between and amid periods of reflection and more conferencing, there was free time, even to sit in the sun and go swimming, if one wished.

It was a new experience for Alice. She was determined that it would consummate her conversion. She thought that her first meditation had gone well, "with the grace of God." At least the time had gone quickly. A statement in her notebook captures the primary agenda of the retreat:

> I have nothing. I can fail, but I am always the song coming from the mouth of God. Whether the [results] are beautiful or poor depends upon how I use the gifts He has given me. . . . All is His except the Will. That is mine to give back to Him—out of love so that I can be totally His.[5]

Long before her conversion, Alice had been searching for peace and an anchor in faith. What would it take to make her really happy? Now she felt she understood why she had not found the happiness she was looking for. Where had she been for the past four years? She had been in hospitals, where there is small opportunity for mortal sins; however, her venial sins had thrived. She had been lost in self-pity, anger, laxity, and, most of all, pride.

She wrote: "What rebellion has grown in my heart? Smug? Complacent? Yes!"[6] Then, upon further reflection, she adds that her greatest sin had been uncharitableness. Hadn't she used her TB as an excuse for impatience, frustration, and irritation—not only for others but for herself as well?

In those vigils, when the Son and the Blessed Virgin seemed omnipresent, even her deep-seated care about her own looks came under her driven scrutiny:

> A woman gets proud of her appearance—her body. She's attractive to gaze upon and knows it. Knows also that others find her so. She is attracted to things that are good to look at—handsome men, a good-looking car, money to spend, polished manners, [and a] glib tongue. [She] can be deceived because she wants to be deceived.[7]

She spent time considering and itemizing the feeling of rebellion that continued to roil within her. She felt rebellion against her family, who seemed to take her for granted, and expected her to arrive whenever there was trouble. Yet she knew, as she thought more honestly about it, that she had encouraged them to rely on her. She felt rebellion against TB, rebellion against people who were telling her what to do—especially men—even in those cases when she knew they were right.

And then there was jealousy and envy. She envied people who had homes, children, and settled lives. As she thought on, she realized that at this time she did not want the attending responsibilities. She wrote: "Would I simply like the rewards without any of the tasks? Probably." It was a thorough grilling and criticism of self—more severe than was necessary—but remarkably, in all that chastisement, Alice was experiencing, a much-needed "rejuvenating process."

At the end of the week, there was no blinding light, no epiphany. Still and all, Alice wrote: "Surely my soul and mind seem relaxed, peaceful and tranquil. I only pray that I can continue to apply some of these things I have absorbed here when I am among people who irritate and annoy me no end. . . . I'm anxious to rid myself of harmful pride . . . [but] I need a starter; I am not original."

Here was a beginning, one of those rare second chances. While she would keep on praying and meditating, she needed to work at something of worth, even if it meant retraining.

During the spring and summer of 1957, when she was enrolled at the Sadie Brown Collegiate Institute, Alice went back to nursing. In the operating room at Garden General Hospital, Garden City, New York, she found that she still had the skills, although the work was exhausting. She also nursed at the Montefiore Hospital in the Bronx, a facility founded by Jewish leaders in the community, and experiencing a growing reputation in the medical world. She still felt called to healing, but it was a matter of endurance. Her personal records reveal that she was "inactive" during the next fall and winter.

Home was still Maine, with her extended family there. She never missed sending a dollar (a big gift in those days) to each niece and nephew on their birthdays, along with special gifts at Christmas. A fringed buckskin jacket arrived for one nephew, and he was king of the neighborhood whenever he wore it.

During the following years, she went back to visit with them all, arriving with her large dangling earrings and in her big Dodge with its aeronautical fins rising above the back bumper. Her nephew was most impressed with the push-button transmission! The young ones would meet her at the door with books for her to read to them. She gave her niece a copy of *Born Free*. They talked about that book and so many other things, such as why *island* is spelled with an "s."

Sometimes she came home because someone in the family needed her help, and her ability to get things done. She knew people, and she still had a reputation as the woman who had served in Bataan and survived Corregidor. Sometimes she arrived for a family get-together at her sister Catherine's camp on Boyd Lake, south of Brownville and Milo, or at her sister Helena's camp at Sebec Lake. The young people would sleep all over the camp, "like cordwood," but before they slept, they pressed their faces between the spokes of the loft railing—listened to their uncle Ken accompanying himself on his ukulele, and watching the grown-ups' shenanigans.

At the Eli Zwicker home in Brownville Junction, there was a piano on the back porch. The family would gather around when Alice came. Sometimes she would play, or sometimes her sister Catherine would, but always it would be the old songs that everyone knew. With Alice came Tana, a big, alert-eared German shepherd. Tana had been Terry and Al Johnson's dog until they left her with Alice while Al was on a tour of duty in Germany. Alice and Tana bonded. Even when resting on the floor, her eyes followed Alice. She would sit by the piano and "sing," as Alice described her contribution, whenever Alice played. When Al and Terry returned to the States, there was no breaking up the pair, so Tana remained Alice's dog.

In all her meditations and introspection, so filled with her own failures and faults, Alice did not mention her abiding gift of sensitivity. She never failed to reach out and become involved in the well-being of others. Like her mother, she was critical, but she was equally ready with accolades when praise was due. Alice had gotten a D in "tact" on her evaluation for a nurse's license, but a B in "courtesy" (a B on those forms was considered a high mark). Courtesy goes deeper and further than tact. She kept her problems largely to herself, just as her father had. She never claimed to be a saint, but her first prayers were for others. She was fun to be with; that was what her young nieces and nephews remember. They loved Aunt Alice.

In 1959, Alice consummated her old dream of buying land in Hawaii.[5] It was just an empty lot in a development, but it provided room for a *vagabond house*—the type of house that Blanding had described in the poem she had treasured ever since those days in Santo Tomas.

For the time being, however, she had moved into rented rooms at the May Basket Motel near Worcester, Massachusetts, and she did so with a glad heart, because it was near Father Mac. In fact, the May Basket was owned by members of his family. It was a neat place built around its own pond and catering to renters rather than one-nighters. One of her nephews remembers visiting his Aunt Alice there. She was taking dancing lessons and dragged him along to one of the sessions.

As Christmas 1962 neared, Alice was disappointed. Father Mac would be in Pensacola, Florida, during the days before the holy festival. He was to accompany a group of Holy Cross ROTC students and work with the personnel of the Aviation Psychology Branch of the Naval School of Aviation Medicine. Alice had not seen her dear friend and spiritual guide often enough that fall; he had spent any available time he'd had with his father, who was dying of cancer. Father Mac left on schedule, and on December 20, he died in his sleep of a massive coronary attack. He was just forty-four.

The president of Holy Cross wrote this about Father Mac: "Words cannot adequately describe his contribution to the intellectual and spiritual life of the campus, nor can they sufficiently express the sense of loss felt by his colleagues and by the students who held him in high esteem for his teaching and his priestly zeal."[9]

Those in Pensacola with whom he had been working sent a telegram to the faculty at Holy Cross, testifying that George McKeon, S.J., was "one of the warmest, most enjoyable, and most stimulating men they had ever met."[10]

For Alice, the whirlwind of darkness had struck again.

Eleven years later, she wrote to her niece: "When he died so suddenly and unexpectedly, only the God who took him has any idea of the utter and complete devastation I experienced. I clung blindly to my faith. I couldn't even pray. It seemed that I had gone mad—but one doesn't." And then Alice gives her niece this advice, gained from having passed through the valley of the shadow of death: "Take it a day at a time, my dearest. We can plan for tomorrow, but we cannot live in it."

Alice's healing came from inside herself.

At the end of that December in which Father Mac died, Alice had a dream. She got up at four-thirty in the morning and wrote down what she remembered.

In the dream she had not recognized the place she was in, nor did she remember how Father Mac arrived, but when he did, he was not alone. Her sister Catherine was with him, and a younger girl with dark hair, whom Alice did not recognize. Later, Alice wondered if this person had come from Limbo; she seemed very glad to have come.

There was never any doubt that Father Mac had died. This was not a return to life but a brief visit. He was dressed in his clerics, smiling his old smile, but with a sense of detachment. He knew all that had transpired since his death. At no time was Alice alone with him, although she told the Father Mac in her dream that she wanted to be. He was ironing and pressing his clothes. (Alice noted that he had done that at her place the last time he had visited, before his death.)

As Alice watched him ironing, there washed over her a feeling that even in his death he was still helping to convert souls. A large group of people had now assembled and were sitting in the next room, waiting for Father Mac to come in and talk to them. Someone was passing out drinks. When Alice said she wanted one, Father Mac told her that she did not need that now, and he kissed her on the cheek. Alice went into the room with the multitude and sat with her sister Geraldine. She awoke with a feeling of peace.

There were several other dreams. In one, Father Mac said, "You'd better talk to me now, Alice, because you know I can't come back like this." Alice adds, "I seemed to *know* that." With these dreams, the acceptance and the healing began.

Alice never did get to Hawaii. There was a place in Maine that became her vagabond house—her cherished camp on a knoll above Bonny Eagle Lake.

She had bought the camp from her uncle Rank Bartlett, one of her mother's railroading brothers, for $1,500, and had managed to come up with the monthly payment of twenty-five dollars. It was just a camp, not a house transplanted to the waterside. It sat as if it belonged in the quiet of the open woods, overlooking the shining lake. It had a kitchen, a bedroom, and a screened-in porch, with a rolled tarp that could be pulled down in foul weather to cover the porch screens. The nieces and nephews would sleep on the porch when the families gathered, lying there and listening to the sounds of dancing in the kitchen, where everything movable had been pushed aside. The jitterbugging went on for hours, with the whispering slide of moccasins (the favorite camp footwear of Alice and her sisters) on the linoleum, while from the Victrola and a 78 record, Tiny Hill's orchestra played tunes such as "Two-Ton Tessie from Nashville," "Tennessee," and "Show Me the Way to Go Home."

Before Father Mac died, he had spent vacations at Bonny Eagle. He took Alice's young nephew fishing out on the lake and told him stories he was not to repeat to his aunt Alice. After Father Mac's death, his memory lingered on at the camp, but it was a happy spirit and did not trouble.

Alice would also spend a great deal of time at Bonny Eagle with her second husband, Frank McAlevey, a man she had met years earlier, but would truly come to know in the 1960s.

Alice wrote in her notebook:

> We had not been able to get to camp until this weekend. We flew up Friday night, back Sunday night, had a car rental. What a joy—like dying and going to heaven—just to get away from it all and *do nothing*. Saturday was a snowy, rainy day, and cozy. Sat before the fire, read, dozed, and just was relaxed! Marvelous! Didn't even watch TV![11]

—✺—

When Alice was a student nurse and doing a rotation at Children's Hospital in Boston, she had met and become close friends with Ann Dunleavy. When Ann married Frank McAlevey, Alice embraced him in her friendship for Ann.

Then, in 1960, Ann was killed in an automobile accident. Her death was another blow. Alice supported Frank as much as she was able and grew closer to him as the years went by. They were married on April 2, 1966, in a brief civil service, and then again on the following June 18 in a Catholic church, with her sister Catherine and her husband as witnesses.

Frank's aunt owned a fine, old white-clapboard house on 8th Street in Brooklyn, New York. It had been a farmhouse before the city grew and the brownstones had crowded around. There was an ample apartment on the second floor, which became Alice and Frank's new home.

According to Eli Zwicker, whose appraisal of people was keen, Frank was a solid man.[12] It took time for him to get to know people, but when and if these preliminaries were accomplished, he was a genuine friend. Although, or perhaps because, Frank could be as blunt as Alice, the relationship worked. Alice wrote of their relationship: "It was like coming into a safe harbor after years on a storm-tossed sea . . . a deep down contented sort of love."[13]

Alice settled down to keeping house in their Brooklyn apartment. Her husband's job was difficult and often stressful, but he always came home to a dinner table set with the best china and silver. Alice could cook, and found new joy in doing things that were immediately deemed valuable and genuinely appreciated.

When Eli's oldest daughter graduated from high school, Alice invited her to visit in Brooklyn, where she could experience the big world. The visit was a success, and Alice planned to entertain each of Eli's five daughters and his son as they graduated. They did the sights: the Statue of Liberty and even Ken's English Chop House, with all the pipes hanging from the ceiling. Aunt Alice taught her niece that if you had to stand on the subway, do so with something solid at your back. This was the city, and one couldn't be too careful. Perhaps it was an overreaction to the danger of being mugged, but deep down there were old habits and fears that the war had lodged in Alice's psyche.

Brooklyn and New York were fine places to visit, but increasingly the camp on Bonny Eagle Lake and Frank's upcoming retirement had more appeal. Alice had looked forward to living in a community again, but

8th Street did not provide the sense of connection Alice had known in Brownville. When the McAleveys' visitors parked on the street, Frank paid a couple of boys to watch the car. Alice's growing dislike of the city took on a larger dimension when she was the victim of a holdup in a beauty parlor, of all places.[14] She and the other victims were forced into a closet and locked in, until they were later rescued by police.

The city did bring out Alice's feistiness. She battled with the city's bureaucracy when an infant shade tree got pushed over by a city truck. She got the tree replaced, and, when the new tree was smaller than the one that had been destroyed, she managed to have it replaced as well. It took a lot of doing, but there was enjoyment in the battle.

Her next cause involved the city's waterworks department when its directors decided that customers would be billed an extra fee to compensate for those who had not paid their water bill. Alice boiled at this proposition. She intended to pay her own water bill, but not the bill of some indigent who had little idea of obligation!

When word came that her mother's health was failing rapidly, Frank had been temporarily disabled by an accident, and for a few days Alice was uncertain whether or not she would be able to get home to be with her mother. Later she wrote to her sister Geraldine:

> I am so glad that I went . . . and was able to spend Saturday night with her. [This was to be her mother's last night.] I believe that she knew I was there by the way she smiled at me once. . . . Helena and I [showed] the nurses some of the snaps of Ma and Dad that we had in our wallets. Ma looked so desperate that we wanted them to realize that she had been a darned nice-looking woman . . . she had such stature, always carried herself well. One could never believe that the figure in that bed was the same woman.[15]

As Alice wrote, there is a deep, unbridgeable finality in the death of one's parents.

Alice and her siblings had known that their mother was very ill. Although she was sometimes difficult in her last years, it was only after she was gone that they realized how much their mother had truly meant to them—how much both Mary and James, in the midst of their own hardships, had given to their children. Only when her mother was laid beside her husband and little James, who had died so many years ago, would Alice feel that her mother was completely at rest, even if "it is just her earthly remains."[16]

Her mother's death was for the best, Alice told herself. Mary Zwicker's reason for being had been having all her family close around her, with her husband always there as her mate, even when he could not be home. Now the family was dispersing, and her husband was gone.

Alice wrote to her sister that their mother had become "like a ship without a rudder." Still and all, Mary's death hit hard. "But, Geddy," Alice wrote to her sister Geraldine, "isn't it wonderful that we can be so pleased with the personal things she left us?"

In 1974, Alice wrote a letter to one of her nieces that drew from a reservoir of resolution.[17] She quoted from the Serenity Prayer, which she had gotten from Alcoholics Anonymous: "God grant me the serenity to accept the things I cannot change, courage to change the things I can."

In secular terms, she had learned that you have to play the hand you are dealt, learning that you cannot "physically, mentally, and spiritually take on the suffering and/or the joy of the universe."

Nor can one do without faith:

> I am not talking about religion, per se, but *Faith,* no matter what your belief may be—God, a Supreme Being, a Higher Being, whatever you choose to call it. . . . We are all self-centered and focus on our [losses]. . . . [T]hink upon the joy you can give. Project out, not in. . . . Be we-centered. . . . There is an old saying that if we shook all the troubles in a basket, we'd still take our own because we don't know whose we might get!

Her niece was worried about a grandmother who was seriously ill. Alice advised, "Make your grandmother chuckle."

Alice shared more benefits gleaned from her experience: "Don't go looking for problems." Writing about learning and pain, she advised: "We can live and learn or we can just live. . . . [E]merge having learned something."

In April of 1974, Alice went to the convention of POWs in Texas. Frank retired, and they went to Bonny Eagle to live year-round. Life had quieted down into a routine, but as 1976 approached, there were ominous hints in her correspondence that she was not feeling well. She had a bowel obstruction in the spring. That condition seemed to improve, but her doctors warned that the problem would return.

Then Alice was diagnosed with ovarian cancer. She danced at the wedding of her brother's daughter, but by the end of June, she had been admitted to the Methodist Hospital in Brooklyn, where she died.[18] She was not quite sixty years old.

The *Quan*, the newsletter for the American Defenders of Bataan and Corregidor, noted her passing:

> The Angels of Bataan and Corregidor lost another of their members on June 28, 1976, when Alice "Swish" Zwicker McAlevey lost her fight after a yearlong bout with cancer. She was a dear person to all who knew her well. We will fondly remember how dearly she loved to dance, sing, and play the piano.[19]

In *Peace of Mind*, the book that Alice so admired, Rabbi Joshua Liebman writes:

> We must make up for the threatened brevity of life by heightening the intensity of life. . . . [Our goal should be] to live fully, richly, nobly, here and now, and make possible a society where other [human beings] can also live.

Alice achieved this view of life, and she would tell us that no island lies beyond the bounds of love and care.

EPILOGUE

Across the cemetery in Brownville, Maine, the breeze carried the soft sound of the Stars and Stripes folding and unfolding on its tall pole. Before me were three smaller American flags beside three military memorial stones, all engraved with the name Zwicker.

The stone at the left reads:

A.N.C.

ALICE ZWICKER MCALEVEY

POW 3 1/2 YEARS MANILA

MAY 7 1942   FEB 5 1945

Alice May Zwicker was swept into dark worlds she did not choose or create, making much of her life seem irredeemably tragic. As I stood there looking down at the stone and the red geranium that decorated her memorial, it occurred to me that none of the three Zwickers commemorated here was a chauvinist. They were too thoughtful, individualistic, and sensitive for such an oversimplification. They came back from the Pacific and from Europe abhorring war because they had lived amid its horror, pain, and waste.

Yet I felt sure that Alice would not leave her story there. The phrase "a dark and wonderful story" from Elizabeth Norman's book, *We Band of Angels*, kept repeating in my mind. Out of the darkness I had sensed in Alice's life, there was nonetheless a celebration of her profession of healing. Suddenly I felt proud of her willingness to take risks. I felt hope in her kindness and in her bristling against injustices, big or small. There was joy in her love of dancing, her lively piano playing, and in her will to smile.

And then what Alice wrote about freedom came to mind:

> If I learned nothing else during those three and a half years in the Philippines, I knew how true were the words of Patrick Henry, "Give me liberty or give me death!" Believe me, there is no substitute for freedom. It is *always* well worth fighting for, no matter how great the odds.

There, in the warmth of the summer sun, and despite the knowledge of the darkness that had filled Alice's life, I felt a new gladness in being part of this human race, which, at its best, is extraordinary.

NOTES

CHAPTER 1. WHERE THE PLEASANT RIVER FLOWS

1. Alice's manuscript account of Corregidor. Zwicker Family Collection. There was no water to spare for washing dishes.

2. Zwicker, Kenneth, *Hard Times without Depression: Growing Up in Maine 1920–1940* (Brownville, ME: Gwilym R. Roberts, 1987), pp. 62–63.

CHAPTER 2. GROWING UP IN BROWNVILLE

1. Catherine Loretta was born in 1913 and James Herbert in 1914. Information provided by Zwicker family member.

2. Letter: Alice to her sister Geraldine, not dated but shortly after Mary Zwicker's death in 1968. Zwicker Family Collection.

3. Mincher, Geraldine Zwicker, "Childhood Memories." Jayne Mincher Winters Collection.

4. Letter: Alice to Jayne Mincher, April 2, 1974. Jayne Mincher Winters Collection.

5. Zwicker, Kenneth, "Child's Christmas Eve: The Most Special of Days." *Hard Times without Depression: Growing Up in Maine 1920–1940* (Brownville, ME: Gwilym R. Roberts, 1987), p. 54.

6. The following is an example of why Principal Williams is remembered: When Reuben Lancaster, one of the junior high boys, got detention, Principal Williams presented him with a short poem that Reuben was to memorize before he could leave for home. Reuben was bright, and the poem was quickly memorized; he did not expect that the subject of the verse would stay with him for a lifetime. The poem reminded the reader that it was a big world out there, and maybe we should not be overly impressed with our own cleverness and importance. Many years later when Mathew Williams died, Reuben repeated the poem to Mathew's son. (Information from Carlson Williams.)

7. Zwicker, Kenneth, "Nations Will Eventually Go Back to Big Kitchens," *Success Takes Many Experiences: Journalism, War and Humor, 1940–1980: Reminiscences* (Marilyn Coy Zwicker, 1998), p. 149.

CHAPTER 3. THE FAR-OFF MAKING OF A WORLD WAR

1. One thinks of wars as caused by greed, the will for power, and the disregard for human worth. However, wars may also be engendered by the stumbling of good resolutions, from the loss of perspective and clarity, and despite the glimmerings of better acts that might have been. (Author's observation.)

2. Bridges, F. N. Robert, *The Testament of Beauty*, I 592.

3. The tunnel was engineered by the U.S. Army Corps of Engineers using one thousand convicts provided by the Philippine Commonwealth, and the blasting was accomplished with TNT in a powder form that had been condemned. (See corregidorisland.com/malinta.html.)

4. In response to this catastrophe, people in the United States poured out aid to the stricken in Japan. A year later and in contrast to this humanitarian gesture, U.S. restrictions to Japanese immigration and talk of the "yellow peril" resulted in great anger in Japan.

5. Typical of the web of associations in the Pacific, the U.S. relationship with China was both complex and longstanding. For some Americans, China was a place where fortunes could be made, but for many more it was a storybook land. For years it had been the place where missionaries practiced their own "open door" policies and those in search of wisdom encountered threads of oriental thought. (Author's observation.)

CHAPTER 4. BECOMING A LADY WITH A LAMP

1. *Bangor Daily News*, editorial, January 10, 2013, p. A4.
2. Reverby, Susan, *Ordered Care: The Dilemma of American Nursing, 1850–1945* (Cambridge University Press, 1987). Reverby argues that the expectation of service has often been manipulated to impede the professional progress of nursing. Her documentation is a necessary as well as sad commentary on what otherwise is one of the noblest expressions of human compassion.
3. Eleanor McNaughton Chase was a special person and influence in Alice's life. (Interview with Zwicker family member.)

CHAPTER 5. WAFTING OF GARDENIA
AND THE ERUPTION OF WAR

1. This number is in contrast to the seventy-five thousand nurses (29 percent of all registered nurses in the United States) who were in the service by the end of the war. (See www.history.army.mil/books/wwii/72-14/72-14.HTM.)
2. Letter: Mildred Manning to author, December 17, 2011.
3. Norman, Elizabeth, *We Band of Angels*, Pocket Books (New York: Simon & Schuster, 1999), p. xv.
4. Monahan, Evelyn, and Neidel-Greenlee, Rosemary, *All This Hell* (Lexington: University of Kentucky Press, 2000), pp. 14–15.
5. "The Service Record of Lt. Alice M. Zwicker, ANC." Zwicker Family Collection. (This is a commercially prepared format to assist veterans in organizing their service experiences.)
6. Norman, *We Band of Angels*, p. 4.
7. Monahan and Neidel-Greenlee, *All This Hell*, p. 8.
8. *Bangor Daily News*, p. 2, March 10 and 11, 1945.
9. "The Service Record of Lt. Alice M. Zwicker." Zwicker Family Collection.
10. Robert Blezard Dameron (Blezard was his mother's maiden name) was born in 1907 in Dallas, Texas. He was sent to Manila in 1939, taken prisoner by the Japanese in 1942, and placed in Santo Tomas internment camp. (Information provided by Zwicker family member.)
11. Letter: Mildred Manning to author, January 7, 2012.

12. Morris, Eric, *Corregidor* (Cooper Square Press, 1981), p. 55.

13. Morrison, Samuel Eliot, *The Rising Sun in the Pacific* (Annapolis, MD: Naval Institute Press, 2010), p. 77.

14. Because of the International Date Line, this would be December 7 in Hawaii.

15. These tags do not appear to have been military dog tags.

CHAPTER 6. A WORLD RED WITH BLOOD AND FIRE

1. Weinstein, Alfred, *Barbed-Wire Surgeon* (New York: Macmillan, 1948), p. 1.

2. Second Lt. Madeline Ullom in the video *We All Came Home.* U.S. Department of Defense.

3. Morrison, Samuel Eliot, *The Rising Sun in the Pacific* (Annapolis, MD: Naval Institute Press, 2010), pp. 170–71.

4. Santa Scholastica's shaded enclosure is boarded on the north and south by Estrada and Pablo Ocampo Streets.

5. War Plan Orange 3 was one of a number of color-coded plans conceived to meet possible invasion. See: Louis Morton, *The War in the Pacific: The Fall of the Philippines* (London: Press Holdings International, 2004), p. 61. Morton makes note that the plan assumed that the Japanese would attack without declaration of war and probably during the dry season of December or January. Many army planners felt that relief would not be possible before the six months of supplies in place ran out.

6. Morris, Eric, *Corregidor: The American Alamo of World War II* (Cooper Square Press, 2000), p. 143.

7. On top of all the exigencies, the stabilizing force of Captain Maude Davison, Chief of Army Nurses in the Philippines, had been temporarily lost. She had sustained a back injury when she was knocked down by a bomb concussion and had to be transferred to Corregidor. Fortunately, her second in command was capable, caring Josephine Nesbit. See Norman, Elizabeth, *We Band of Angels*, Pocket Books (New York: Simon & Schuster, 1999), p. 22.

8. Dr. Weinstein's admiration of Frances Nash's ability as a nurse may have gone back to his younger professional days in Atlanta. (Author's observation.)

9. General MacArthur proclaimed Manila an "open city," hoping to reduce the destruction of further attack. (See history.army.mil/books/wwii/5-2/5-2_14.htm.)

10. Alice and several other evacuees reported that as they crossed Manila Bay on the night of the 26th, they could see either the flash of bombs or fires

burning on Corregidor. However, records indicate that the first bombing of the "Rock" did not begin until December 29. The remaining Army nurses with the exception of one assigned to the ship *Mactan* were evacuated on December 29 and 30. Eleven navy nurses remained isolated at Santa Scholastica. They were there when the Japanese entered the hospital on January 2.

CHAPTER 7. BATAAN

1. Many sources mention the nipa-thatched roofs of Hospital No. 1. However, Dr. Weinstein describes the barrack buildings as being clapboarded and having metal roofs. There is general agreement that the buildings were "dilapidated." As the site was destroyed by the Japanese, many questions regarding this facility remain. The description given in this text draws largely from the accounts of Weinstein, Nurse Juanita Redmond, Alice, and a diagram of the hospital layout from the National Archives provided by the General Douglas MacArthur Foundation.

2. In the final weeks of the defense, the combat efficiency was reduced more than 75 percent. Surgeon of Luzon Force Report II, Medical, Supply and Personnel. Internet.

3. The first group of casualties appear to have numbered 212.

4. Glusman, John A., *Conduct Under Fire* (New York: Viking, 2005), p. 113.

5. Hospital No. 2 was established closer to the southern coast of Bataan and on the Real River. It's initial task was to attend to medical cases and the surgical overflow from Hospital No. 1.

6. The Battles of the Points and the Pockets refer to fighting on the rugged, western coast of Bataan. See the Map of Bataan in the photospread.

7. Monahan, Evelyn, and Neidel-Greenlee, Rosemary, *All This Hell* (Lexington: University of Kentucky Press, 2000), p. 41. This account states that Hospital No. 1 did 425 operations in thirty-six hours.

8. Weinstein, Alfred A., *Barbed-Wire Surgeon: A Prisoner of War in Japan* (New York: Macmillan, 1948), p. 20.

9. Redmond, Juanita, *I Served on Bataan* (Philadelphia: Lippincott Williams, & Wilkins, 1943), p. 144.

10. Dr. John Bumgarner, in his *Parade of the Dead* (Jefferson, NC: McFarland, 2004), blames the plague of "big blue flies" that bred around the latrines for the spreading of the intestinal diseases in the hospitals. In the field there was another cause. The dust and thirst drove men to drink polluted water.

11. Glusman, *Conduct Under Fire*, p. 136.

12. Norman, Elizabeth, *We Band of Angels*, Pocket Books (New York: Simon & Schuster, 1999), p. 77.

13. Morton, Louis, *The War in the Pacific: The Fall of the Philippines* (London: Press Holdings International, 2004), p. 379. Even in the hospitals, sanitation was far from ideal. The hospital waste was emptied into latrine pits, and the stench at times was so offensive that men relieved themselves elsewhere. Despite the efforts of the nurses to keep hospital areas sanitary, one doctor thought that there were "many cross infections."

14. An example of the Japanese losses is given in Louis Morton's description of "The Battle of the Points," *The War in the Pacific*, chapter 17. In this series of engagements even the heavy coastal guns of Corregidor added their deadly toll.

15. Morris, Eric, *Corregidor: The American Alamo of World War II* (Cooper Square Press, 2000), p. 370.

16. Dr. Alfred Weinstein notes in his *Barbed-Wire Surgeon*, p. 10, that Duckworth was not loved by those under him but was "respected and obeyed."

17. As in the case of the hospital at Limay, these buildings were variously described. The description here is based on a plan from the National Archives along with information from several other sources including Weinstein and Redmond's *I Served in Bataan*.

18. Brantley, Hattie, "The Flight of the Army Nurse Corps," *Ex-POW Bulletin* 32, February 1975, p. 3.

19. Weinstein, *Barbed-Wire Surgeon*, p. 27 and p. 31.

20. Ibid. p. 26. "How and where Fraley [Fraleigh] and his gang got the necessary wood, nails, bolts and tools to finish the job, I'm not quite sure. I believe he employed a combination of barter, soft soap, hospital alcohol, and outright thievery."

21. Alice's brother Ken, who knew her better than anyone else, was sure that his sister was truly in love with her Lt. Fred Newell. We do not know whether Alice saw him after the *Maryanne* sailed out into a black Manila Bay. Early in May 1942, the *Maryanne* was destroyed to keep her out of Japanese hands. Newell was captured with the fall of Corregidor.

22. Weinstein locates this swimming party as being held at "Seseman Cove" on the bay facing Corregidor. The army topographical map of this area shows a "Sisiman Cove" east and across from Port Mariveles. It also fills the description by facing Corregidor. (Author's observation.)

23. *Bangor Daily News*, March 5, 1945.

24. Juanita Redmond was one of the few nurses retrieved by plane from Corregidor before that fortress surrendered. Doubtless encouraged, she lost no time in getting her book, *I Served on Bataan*, into print. The story of Alice and the foxhole is contained in this book (pp. 118–20) and was the source for an item in the *Bangor Daily News*, April 15, 1943. The Zwickers were thrilled to get any news of Alice. Later, they came to feel Redmond had been self-serving in her treatment of the foxhole incident. (From interviews with members of Zwicker family.)

25. Lukacs, John, *Escape from Davao: The Forgotten Story of the Most Daring Prison Escape of the Pacific War* (New York: NAL Trade, 2011), p. 50.

26. The size of the bomb is variously reported. Some sources report five hundred pounds while others one thousand pounds.

27. Redmond in *I Served in Bataan* conflates the two bombings on Hospital No. 1, but her descriptions are firsthand and graphic.

28. Norman, *We Band of Angels*, p. 87.

29. Brantley, "The Flight of the Army Nurse Corps," p. 34.

30. Alice notes that there was a "bomber's moon" that night.

31. Norman, *We Band of Angels*, p. 88.

32. Weinstein, *Barbed-Wire Surgeon*, p. 66.

CHAPTER 8. CORREGIDOR

1. Morris, Eric, *Corregidor: The American Alamo of World War II* (Cooper Square Press, 2000), p. 30.

2. The United States took the Washington Naval Treaty seriously and limited military building in the Pacific to support facilities.

3. Bentley, Hattie, 1983 ANC interview. Quoted in Elizabeth Norman's *We Band of Angels*, Pocket Books (New York: Simon & Schuster, 1999), p. 100.

4. Morton, Lewis, *The War in the Pacific: The Fall of the Philippines* (London: Press Holdings International, 2004), p. 542.

5. Morris, *Corregidor*, p. 293.

6. Norman, Elizabeth, *We Band of Angels*, Pocket Books (New York: Simon & Schuster, 1999), p. 98. On page 101 Professor Norman gives a graphic description of conditions in the tunnels as weeks went on.

7. Alice was often considered a Bangor nurse because she was trained in that city. (Author's observation.)

8. Ann Bernatitus was a navy nurse who was evacuated from Corregidor on May 3, 1942.

9. It is likely that the converted yacht that took the nurses from Corregidor to rendezvous with the *Spearfish* was commanded by Alice's friend Lt. Fred Newell. (Author's observation.)

10. Letter: Ann Bernatitus to Mary Zwicker. Not dated but probably the end of May 1942. Zwicker Family Collection.

11. This horrible incident that left the nurses aghast, despite all they had seen, is described in many sources including *We Band of Angels*, p. 101, Monahan, and Neidel-Greenlee, *All This Hell*, p. 78.

12. The Japanese landed on the night of Tuesday, May 5, 1942.

13. The amount of explosives poured down on Corregidor is difficult to comprehend. It is reported that on April 29, the day of Emperor Hirohito's birthday, one hundred tons of bombs and ten thousand artillery shells smashed Corregidor. See also: Wainwright, Jonathan, *General Wainwright's Story* (Garden City, NY: Doubleday & Company, 1946), for extensive figures on explosives received by Corregidor.

14. The concussions were debilitating. Clark Lee, an Associated Press correspondent, wrote that the concussions "drove all intelligence from the nurses' eyes and left them vacant and staring."

15. In those last hours, the main tunnel was so jammed with military and civilian people that one could scarcely move. In the headquarters lateral, there was a scramble to destroy maps and papers. Outside the tunnel, it was a brave and bloody shambles. Once the Japanese had tanks ashore, they advanced relentlessly. The cost in lives on both sides leaves one shuddering.

16. From a typed manuscript written by Alice and found among her belongings by her nephew Rodney Tenney.

17. Colonel Wibb Cooper, the American chief medical officer, later convinced the Japanese to let the prisoners bury the bodies because they were a health hazard.

CHAPTER 9. SANTO TOMAS

1. The nurses' fear for their patients' well-being was well founded. The men in the ship's hold were given neither water nor food.

2. Ullom, Madeline, "ANC Interview." As quoted by Elizabeth Norman, *We Band of Angels*, p. 141.

3. The committee was originally called the American Coordinating Committee. This background on the Santo Tomas Internment Camp comes from Frederic Stevens's *Santo Tomas Internment Camp* (New York: Stratford House, 1946).

4. It is probable that the Japanese had considered using Santo Tomas as an internment camp before they captured Luzon and Manila.

5. Norman, *We Band of Angels*, pp. 150–52.

6. Account of Lt. Hattie Brantley. See Monahan, Evelyn, and Neidel-Greenlee, Rosemary, *All This Hell* (Lexington: University of Kentucky Press, 2000), p. 99.

7. Nurse Peggy Greenwalt had in her bag the unit colors for the 12th Regiment of the Quartermaster Corps. It had been solemnly given to her when Corregidor fell with the hope she might be able to get it back to the states. There was a tense moment when a puzzled Japanese soldier, who had been going through Peggy's bag, held up the flag. Lt. Greenwalt took the flag and wrapped it around her shoulders with a smile. The shawl ruse worked, and in time the 12th Regiment's flag got home. (See Elizabeth Norman's *We Band of Angels*, p. 152.)

8. Other names on the birthday card were Marie Atkinson (a woman imprisoned with the nurses), Eleanor Lee, and Letha McHale. Zwicker Family Collection.

9. Letters: Mildred Manning to the author, August 2011.

10. The subcommittee on medicine was headed by Dr. Charles Leach, who had been on his way to China when war broke out. He had been placed in Santo Tomas, where he and the navy nurses from Santa Scholastica had established medical facilities.

11. In writing this, the author is indebted to Elizabeth Norman, who with great skill coalesced in her *We Band of Angels* the memories of many nurses.

12. Stevens, *Santo Tomas Internment Camp*, p. 29 and following.

13. In addition to these causes of friction, there was the issue of whether Davison still legitimately held the position of command.

14. Powers, Alice Hahn, "Interview of Nurses," 1983, Center for Military History.

15. Letter: Dorothy Davis to Mary Zwicker, December 4, 1943. Miss Davis was a non-military nurse who was exchanged and returned to the United States onboard the Swedish ship *Gripsholm*. At Santo Tomas she joined with six other nurses, including Alice, to supplement their diet.

16. Information taken from Stevens's *Santo Tomas Internment Camp*, pp. 227–31. At first each shanty group had a mayor; later each cluster of shanties had a supervisor.

17. See Monahan and Neidel-Greenlee, *All This Hell*, pp. 109–10. The Red Cross medical supplies, which arrived on the day after Christmas 1942, were kept by the Japanese.

18. See Monahan and Neidel-Greenlee's *All This Hell*, pp. 109–10, and Norman's *We Band of* Angels, p. 154.

19. *Bangor Daily News*, December 1942. The Zwickers received an official notice dated March 10, 1943, from the Adjutant General's Office stating that Alice was a prisoner of war in the Philippine Islands. Zwicker Family Collection.

20. The booklet features an Easter Mass celebrated in the Cathedral of St. Mary and St. John which was associated with Santo Tomas. Zwicker Family Collection.

21. Alice's book list is found in an appropriated Philippine Bureau of Education notebook in which she kept other lists; copied poems, passages, and witty sayings; and kept study notes. Zwicker Family Collection.

22. Along with the citing of Caldwell's book, Alice also gives the text from Matthew 28:24. "For wheresoever the carcass is, there will the eagles gather together."

23. The homemade booklet is composed in part of 8" × 11" sheets of paper with the letterhead of the United States Commissioner of the Philippine Islands. Perhaps Alice had picked up this paper while in Malinta Tunnel. Zwicker Family Collection.

24. Don Blanding was born in Oklahoma. He enlisted in both WWI and WWII, traveled widely, and became known as the poet laureate of Hawaii. (Author's observation.)

25. On the second notebook, Alice wrote "Japanese" in the blank for the teacher's name, evidently referring to the negative influence of her captors.

26. Stevens, *Santo Tomas Internment Camp*, p. 188.

27. Woodcock, Teedie Cowie, *Behind the Sawali: Santo Tomas in Cartoons, 1942–1945* (Greensboro, NC: Cenografix, 2000), p. 54.

28. Quoted from Stevens's *Santo Tomas Internment Camp*.

29. Alice's interview in the *Bangor Daily News*, March 5, 1945.

30. Woodcock, *Behind the Sawali*.

31. Alice's interview in the *Bangor Daily News*, March 5, 1945.

32. Letter: Mildred Dalton to author.

33. Alice's own medical notes indicate that the fluoroscope examination showed calcified spots. The facility at which this examination took place is not

given. There is no information on the second occasion in which Alice left the camp. Zwicker Family Collection.

34. Alice's interview in the *Bangor Daily News*, March 5, 1945.

35. Ibid.

36. Carroll, Earl, *The Secret Story of Santo Tomas*, chapter 2, *Los Angeles Examiner*, 1945.

37. The reference here is to local radio. The Japanese suspected and searched for a radio that would have brought in world news. While such a radio did exist, it was never found by the Japanese. (Author's observation.)

38. Carroll, *The Secret Story of Santo Tomas*, chapter 3.

39. Alice's address to the Kiwanis Club in Dover-Foxcroft as reported in the *Piscataquis Observer*, March 1945.

40. Zwicker, Alice, "Testimony before the Committee on War Crimes," July 24, 1945, 11–45 363 (40–31), National Archives, College Park, Maryland.

41. Nash, Frances L., "Georgia Nurse's Own Story," *Atlantic Journal Magazine*, p. 6, April 22, 1945.

42. Zwicker, "Testimony before Committee on War Crimes." Alice gives her total weight loss as thirty-five pounds.

43. Ibid. Alice testifies that she never saw any medical supplies provided directly from the Japanese.

CHAPTER 10. LIBERATION AND HOME

1. Alice's testimony before the War Crimes Committee and her interview in the *Bangor Daily News* published on March 5, 1945.

2. Norman, Elizabeth, *We Band of Angels*, p. 198.

3. Nash, Frances L., "Georgia Nurse's Own Story," *Atlantic Journal Magazine*, p. 2, 2–3 September 1945.

4. Young, Eunice, Diary, 1941–1945, as quoted by Monahan, Evelyn, and Neidel-Greenlee, *All This Hell*, p. 152.

5. There is evidence that as the American forces closed in, the fanatical element of the Imperial Army issued detailed directions on how the allied prisoners were to be destroyed. Alice testified before the War Crimes Commission that her close friend Chief Petty Officer Edward McIntosh, who had been a prisoner at Bilibid Prison Camp, had stated that he had knowledge that this camp was "mined by the Japanese for the purpose of killing the prisoners." (Memorandum in records of the Judge Advocate General, War Crimes Branch, case file 40-33-208, 26 July, 1945.)

6. Wygle, Peter R., "Santo Tomas Raid," *Saber*, January/February, 2005.

7. Information taken from A. V. H. Hardendorp's *The Santo Tomas Story*, edited from F. H. Golay's *The Official History of the Santo Tomas Internment Camp* (New York: McGraw-Hill, 1946). How deeply the hatred for the Japanese military ran is illustrated in the treatment of Lt. Akibo as he was dragged to the aid station in the Santo Tomas main building. He was kicked, spit upon, and even burned with cigarettes.

8. Six American soldiers had been killed in taking Santo Tomas.

9. Meier, Rose Rieper, Department of Defense Interview, 1984.

10. Alice took the helmet home, and it hung on the wall of her camp at Bonny Eagle Lake in Maine for many years.

11. From a newspaper article written by Brian S. McNiff, the *Gazette,* undated. Zwicker Family Collection.

12. *Bangor Daily News*, February 7, 1951.

13. Letter: Alice to the *New York Daily News*, January 22, 1973.

14. Stevens, *Santo Tomas Internment Camp*, p. 380. It was difficult for the Americans to silence the enemy guns. One was placed on the rooftop of the Philippine General Hospital.

15. Alice remembered the plane as a C-54, which is a four-engine craft that could carry up to eighty personnel, but this plane seems too large for landing and taking off from a city boulevard. Most accounts report that the plane was a C-47, which is corroborated by photos taken of nurses boarding in Manila. (Author's observation.)

16. Nestor, Helen Cassiani, Department of Defense Interview, 1983.

17. Information from Elizabeth Norman's *We Band of Angels*.

18. Other decorations to follow were the Asiatic-Pacific Theater Ribbon with two bronze stars, the American Theater Ribbon, the World War II Victory Medal, and the Philippine Defense Ribbon with bronze star.

19. Alice's interview in the *Bangor Daily News*, March 5, 1945.

20. Norman, *We Band of Angels*, p. 219.

21. Accounts of the arrival of the nurses in California differ. As a primary source, the author has used information provided in the March 3, 1945, issue of the Letterman General Hospital's *Fog Horn*.

22. Letter: Mildred Manning to author, March 2012.

23. *Bangor Daily News*, special feature by Nelle Penley, March 5, 1945.

24. Ibid.

25. Telegrams in the Zwicker Family Collection.

CHAPTER 11. LIMELIGHT

1. *Bangor Daily News*, special feature by Nelle Penley, March 5, 1945.
2. Ibid.
3. By necessity the dinner was by invitation and the following reception open to the public. (Author's note.)
4. From clippings in Alice's scrapbook; neither the sources nor dates are identified. They are probably from the *Bangor Daily News*.
5. President Hauck of the University of Maine was also chairman of the Penobscot Chapter of the Red Cross.
6. "Lieut. Alice Zwicker Charms Audience at Red Cross Rally," *Bangor Daily News*, p. 2, March 10–11, 1945.
7. Alice's feeling in making this statement may not have been so much a matter of savage revenge as the fact that the bomb saved the lives of perhaps half a million American soldiers, including her dear brother Ken (per conversation with Alice's brother, Eli Zwicker.)
8. Hogan, Rosemary, "What Did Not Happen to Bataan Nurses," *Liberty*, pp. 80–82, November 17, 1945.
9. *Bangor Daily News*, March 10–11, 1945.
10. Letter: Alice to her sister Geraldine, 1968. Jayne Mincher Winters Collection.
11. Ibid.
12. *Lewiston Evening Journal*, April 20, 1945.
13. *Bangor Daily News*, April 20, 1945
14. Brewster and his fellow legislators were also faced with the issue of drafting nurses. (Author's observation.)
15. Letters: Mary Zwicker to Alice, June 23, 1943, and July 28, 1943. Zwicker Family Collection.
16. "Al" and "Swish" are nicknames for Alice that Ken uses when writing to his sister.
17. Letter: Ken Zwicker to Alice, Okinawa, June 5, 1945. Zwicker Family Collection.

CHAPTER 12. NEW WINGS AND DELUGE

1. Lt. Newell appears to have lost his life on December 15, 1944, in the bombing of the Oryoku off Olongapo in Subic Bay. See oryokumaruonline .org/n.html.

2. Alice reported to Loring AFB on June 24, 1945. Alice's Service Record.

3. One of the lesser known feats of World War II was the airlifting of some 209 sled dogs from various Arctic Rescue Stations to the snow-buried Battle of the Bulge. (Author's observation.)

4. Manuscript narrative written by the public relation officer, 1380th Army Air Force Base Unit, Air Transport Command. Zwicker Family Collection.

5. Frank Stanton's "Keep A-Goin'" was one of Alice's favorite poems. List of favorite poems in one of Alice's notebooks. Zwicker Family Collection.

6. Alice was posted to the 1380th Army Air Force Base Unit stationed at Loring. Alice's Service Record.

7. Letter: Kenneth Zwicker to Alice, July 10, 1945. Zwicker Family Collection.

8. The description of Bataan and Corregidor written by Alice may have been intended for her proposed book. No other manuscript for this book has been found. (Author's observation.)

9. Alice received flight nurse certificate number 377. Certificate is in Zwicker collection at Brownville Historical Society.

10. Records are not clear at this point. Alice and Bob Dameron may have been married at this time. If so, it was a secret union. It is known that Alice wanted a formal service when it was possible. Information provided by Zwicker family member.

11. *Bangor Daily News* and *Piscataquis Observer,* January 2, 1945.

12. Letter: James Zwicker to Alice, Brownville, ME, January 14, 1947. Zwicker Family Collection.

13. Letter: Kenneth Zwicker to Alice, Orono, ME, January 21, 1947. Zwicker Family Collection.

14. From Alice's "Service Record of Lt. Alice May Zwicker, ANC." Zwicker Family Collection.

15. Alice flew to Bangor on Northeast Airlines on February 10, 1948. *Bangor Daily News,* February 13, 1948.

16. *Piscataquis Observer,* May 12, 1948.

17. From Alice's "Service Record of Lt. Alice May Zwicker, ANC." Zwicker Family Collection.

CHAPTER 13. THROUGH THE VALLEY OF THE SHADOW

1. Letter: Alice to Kenneth Zwicker, March 26, [1949]. Zwicker Family Collection.

2. No more information on Alice's friend Ruth has been found.

3. Probably San Diego State College. (Author's observation.)

4. The "I Am Activity" or Saint Germain Foundation was a movement begun by Guy W. Ballard in the late 1920s. Its basic tenet was that every individual possessed a divine spark of the "I am" or God. Its mission was to assist its members in ascending into the presence of the Masters, who included Jesus and Saint Germain. Those failing to ascend to the Godhead would be reincarnated until this goal was reached. (Author's observation.)

5. There is a persistent perception in the Zwicker family that unfaithfulness as well as fear of TB was involved in Dameron's desertion of Alice. If this is the case, then it may explain why Alice felt "hate" toward Dameron at one time. (Informations from Zwicker family members.)

6. Letter: Alice to Kenneth Zwicker, March 26 [1949]. Zwicker Family Collection.

7. See article in the *Journal of Clinical Psychology*, vol. 2, issue 4, October 1946, written by Captain Herbert E. Rubin MC and 2nd Lt. Elias Katz of Crile General Hospital. It would seem that while no controlled testing of Auroratone was made, a number of the created films were shown to patients with the results that patients "became more accessible."

8. See "Auroratone" on YouTube for a presentation of Bing Crosby singing "When the Mighty Organ Played 'Oh, Promise Me'" (also www.youtube.com/watch?v=uFXku4MntpY).

9. Letter: Kenneth Zwicker to Alice, Orono, ME, March 18, 1949. Zwicker Family Collection.

10. Liebman, Joshua L., *Peace of Mind: Insights on Human Nature That Can Change Your Life* (New York: Citadel Press, 1999 [1946]).

11. Ibid., p. xiii, p. 12, and p. 20.

12. The name of this organization had been changed from Bataan Veteran's Organization with the aim of being more inclusive.

13. Letter: Alice to Ken Day. Reprinted in an unidentified newspaper and dated 1950. Zwicker Family Collection.

14. Alice uses the term "pneumothorax," which is a condition when air or gas collects in the pleural space between the lung and the wall of the chest cavity. She may be referring to the treatment of this condition that may involve the collapsing of a lung.

15. Report of the chief of special services dealing with the radio room, March 24, 1952. The name of the institution is not given. Zwicker Family Collection.

16. Letter: Major William C. Taggart, Chaplain 31st Infantry Regiment, to Alice, January 15, 1953. Zwicker Family Collection.

17. The Reverend George McKeon was born in Somerville, Massachusetts, May 7, 1918, graduated from Boston College High School in 1935, studied at Holy Cross 1935–1937 and Catholic University 1945–1946. The author is indebted to Holy Cross and its archivist for information regarding The Reverend George McKeon.

18. Letter: Alice to Jayne Mincher, undated but probably 1974. Jayne Mincher Winters Collection.

19. Scannell, Joseph S., *New England Province News*. College of the Holy Cross, Archives and Special Records, Worcester, MA.

20. The Reverend George J. McKeon, S.J., was a guest lecturer and seminar leader at the Maine Sanatorium in Fairfield, about the time that Alice learned the removal of a lung was her best chance for recovery. However there is no direct evidence that Alice was ever a patient at the Maine Sanatorium. (Author's observation.)

CHAPTER 14. AND YET THE DANCE

1. Letter: Alice to James Mealey, Brownville, January 7, 1954. Jane Macomber Collection.

2. Letter: Alice to James Mealey, Bergstrom AFB, Austin, TX, February 7, 1955. Jane Macomber Collection.

3. Letter: Alice to President Eisenhower, April 8, 1955. Zwicker Family Collection.

4. John Provoo was born in California and early became a student of Buddhism and the Japanese language. Joining the U.S. Army, he was stationed as a clerk at the army headquarters in the Philippines. Taken prisoner, he was accused of using his ability to speak Japanese to rise in favor and influence with the prison camp's administration. After the war, his conviction for treason was overturned by a court of appeals on technical grounds and the claim that his alleged homosexuality had prejudiced the jury. (Information from article on John David Provoo on Wikipedia.)

5. Alice kept notes on the retreat at Lady Isle and on subsequent personal meditations in a blue bound notebook dated 1955–1956. Zwicker Family Collection.

6. Ibid.

7. Ibid.

8. Letter: Innis Arden Realty to Alice, December 17, 1959. Alice placed a down payment on a lot in Hawaii with this company.

9. *Alumnus*, Holy Cross College, February 1963.

10. Obituary by Joseph S. Scannell, S.J., *New England Province News.*

11. Letter: Alice to Jayne Mincher, written around 1974. Jayne Mincher Winters Collection.

12. Frank was well established and supervisor for the New York Tunnel Authority.

13. Letter: Alice to Jayne Mincher, written around 1974. Jayne Mincher Winters Collection.

14. Some family members remember that the robbery took place in a doctor's office; perhaps there were two occasions.

15. Letter: Alice to her sister Geraldine, undated but probably 1968. Zwicker Family collection.

16. One has a better glimpse of Frank McAlevey's character when one knows that he put one thousand dollars in Alice's bank account to cover her mother's funeral and burial expenses.

17. Letter: Alice to Jayne Mincher, not dated but probably the spring of 1974. Jayne Mincher Winter's Collection.

18. Alice died on June 28, 1976, and was buried at Holy Cross Cemetery in Brooklyn alongside of Frank McAlevey's first wife, Ann. Frank, who passed away in 2004, is also buried there.

19. *Quan*, September 1976.